# Flinn Scientific
# ChemTopic™ Labs

# Chemical Reactions

### Senior Editor

**Irene Cesa**
Flinn Scientific, Inc.
Batavia, IL

### Curriculum Advisory Board

**Bob Becker**
Kirkwood High School
Kirkwood, MO

**Kathleen J. Dombrink**
McCluer North High School
Florissant, MO

**Robert Lewis**
Downers Grove North High School
Downers Grove, IL

**John G. Little**
St. Mary's High School
Stockton, CA

**Lee Marek**
University of Illinois–Chicago
Chicago, IL

**John Mauch**
Braintree High School
Braintree, MA

**Dave Tanis**
Grand Valley State University
Allendale, MI

**FLINN SCIENTIFIC INC.**
"Your Safer Source for Science Supplies"
P.O. Box 219 • Batavia, IL 60510
1-800-452-1261 • www.flinnsci.com

ISBN 1-877991-74-0

Copyright © 2004 Flinn Scientific, Inc.

All rights reserved. No part of this book may be reproduced or transmitted in any form or by any means, electronic or mechanical, including, but not limited to photocopy, recording, or any information storage and retrieval system, without permission in writing from Flinn Scientific, Inc.
No part of this book may be included on any Web site.

Reproduction permission is granted only to the science teacher who has purchased this volume of Flinn ChemTopic™ Labs, Chemical Reactions, Catalog No. AP6596 from Flinn Scientific, Inc. Science teachers may make copies of the reproducible student pages for use only by their students.

Printed in the United States of America.

## Table of Contents

| | Page |
|---|---|
| Flinn ChemTopic™ Labs Series Preface | i |
| About the Curriculum Advisory Board | ii |
| Chemical Reactions Preface | iii |
| Format and Features | iv–v |
| Experiment Summaries and Concepts | vi–vii |

### *Experiments*

| | |
|---|---|
| Classifying Chemical Reactions | 1 |
| Double Replacement Reactions and Solubility | 17 |
| A Four-Reaction Copper Cycle | 35 |
| Chemical Reactions and Qualitative Analysis | 49 |

### *Demonstrations*

| | |
|---|---|
| Chemical Reactions Primer | 65 |
| Colorful Electrolysis | 70 |
| The Chef | 73 |
| Foiled Again! | 77 |
| The Yellow and Blue Switcheroo | 81 |
| Old Foamey | 85 |
| Cool Light | 87 |

### *Supplementary Information*

| | |
|---|---|
| Safety and Disposal Guidelines | 90 |
| National Science Education Standards | 92 |
| Master Materials Guide | 94 |

Flinn ChemTopic™ Labs — Chemical Reactions

# Flinn ChemTopic™ Labs Series Preface
## Lab Manuals Organized Around Key Content Areas in Chemistry

In conversations with chemistry teachers across the country, we have heard a common concern. Teachers are frustrated with their current lab manuals, with experiments that are poorly designed and don't teach core concepts, with procedures that are rigid and inflexible and don't work. Teachers want greater flexibility in their choice of lab activities. As we further listened to experienced master teachers who regularly lead workshops and training seminars, another theme emerged. Master teachers mostly rely on collections of experiments and demonstrations they have put together themselves over the years. Some activities have been passed on like cherished family recipe cards from one teacher to another. Others have been adapted from one format to another to take advantage of new trends in microscale equipment and procedures, technology innovations, and discovery-based learning theory. In all cases the experiments and demonstrations have been fine-tuned based on real classroom experience.

Flinn Scientific has developed a series of lab manuals based on these "cherished recipe cards" of master teachers with proven excellence in both teaching students and training teachers. Created under the direction of an Advisory Board of award-winning chemistry teachers, each lab manual in the Flinn ChemTopic™ Labs series contains 4–6 student-tested experiments that focus on essential concepts and applications in a single content area. Each lab manual also contains 4–6 demonstrations that can be used to illustrate a chemical property, reaction, or relationship and will capture your students' attention. The experiments and demonstrations in the Flinn ChemTopic™ Labs series are enjoyable, highly focused, and will give students a real sense of accomplishment.

*Laboratory experiments* allow students to experience chemistry by doing chemistry. Experiments have been selected to provide students with a crystal-clear understanding of chemistry concepts and encourage students to think about these concepts critically and analytically. Well-written procedures are guaranteed to work. Reproducible data tables teach students how to organize their data so it is easily analyzed. Comprehensive teacher notes include a master materials list, solution preparation guide, complete sample data, and answers to all questions. Detailed lab hints and teaching tips show you how to conduct the experiment in your lab setting and how to identify student errors and misconceptions before students are led astray.

*Chemical demonstrations* provide another teaching tool for seeing chemistry in action. Because they are both visual and interactive, demonstrations allow teachers to take students on a journey of observation and understanding. Demonstrations provide additional resources to develop central themes and to magnify the power of observation in the classroom. Demonstrations using discrepant events challenge student misconceptions that must be broken down before new concepts can be learned. Use demonstrations to introduce new ideas, illustrate abstract concepts that cannot be covered in lab experiments, and provide a spark of excitement that will capture student interest and attention.

## Safety, flexibility, and choice

Safety always comes first. Depend on Flinn Scientific to give you upfront advice and guidance on all safety and disposal issues. Each activity begins with a description of the hazards involved and the necessary safety precautions to avoid exposure to these hazards. Additional safety, handling, and disposal information is also contained in the teacher notes.

The selection of experiments and demonstrations in each Flinn ChemTopic™ Labs manual gives you the flexibility to choose activities that match the concepts your students need to learn. No single teacher will do all of the experiments and demonstrations with a single class. Some experiments and demonstrations may be more helpful with a beginning-level class, while others may be more suitable with an honors class. All of the experiments and demonstrations have been keyed to national content standards in science education.

## Chemistry is an experimental science!

Whether they are practicing key measurement skills or searching for trends in the chemical properties of substances, all students will benefit from the opportunity to discover chemistry by doing chemistry. No matter what chemistry textbook you use in the classroom, Flinn ChemTopic™ Labs will help you give your students the necessary knowledge, skills, attitudes, and values to be successful in chemistry.

# About the Curriculum Advisory Board

Flinn Scientific is honored to work with an outstanding group of dedicated chemistry teachers. The members of the Flinn ChemTopic Labs Advisory Board have generously contributed their proven experiments and demonstrations to create these topic lab manuals. The wisdom, experience, creativity, and insight reflected in their lab activities guarantee that students who perform them will be more successful in learning chemistry. On behalf of all chemistry teachers, we thank the Advisory Board members for their service and dedication to chemistry education.

**Bob Becker** teaches chemistry and AP chemistry at Kirkwood High School in Kirkwood, MO. Bob received his B.A. from Yale University and M.Ed. from Washington University and has 20 years of teaching experience. A well-known demonstrator, Bob has conducted more than 100 demonstration workshops across the U.S. and Canada and was a Team Leader for the Flinn Foundation Summer Workshop Program. His creative and unusual demonstrations have been published in the *Journal of Chemical Education,* the *Science Teacher,* and *Chem13 News*. Bob is the author of two books of chemical demonstrations, *Twenty Demonstrations Guaranteed to Knock Your Socks Off, Volumes I and II,* published by Flinn Scientific. Bob has been awarded the James Bryant Conant Award in High School Teaching from the American Chemical Society, the Regional Catalyst Award from the Chemical Manufacturers Association, and the Tandy Technology Scholar Award.

**Kathleen J. Dombrink** teaches chemistry and advanced-credit college chemistry at McCluer North High School in Florissant, MO. Kathleen received her B.A. in Chemistry from Holy Names College and M.S. in Chemistry from St. Louis University and has 35 years of teaching experience. Recognized for her strong support of professional development, Kathleen has been selected to participate in the Fulbright Memorial Fund Teacher Program in Japan and NEWMAST and Dow/NSTA Workshops. She served as co-editor of the inaugural issues of *Chem Matters* and was a Woodrow Wilson National Fellowship Foundation Chemistry Team Member for 11 years. Kathleen is currently a Team Leader for the Flinn Foundation Summer Workshop Program. Kathleen has received the Presidential Award, the Midwest Regional Teaching Award from the American Chemical Society, the Tandy Technology Scholar Award, and a Regional Catalyst Award from the Chemical Manufacturers Association.

**Robert Lewis** recently retired from teaching chemistry at Downers Grove North High School in Downers Grove, IL, and is currently a Secondary Coordinator for the GATE program in Chicago. Robert received his B.A. from North Central College and M.A. from University of the South and has 30 years of teaching experience. He was a founding member of Weird Science, a group of chemistry teachers that traveled throughout the country to stimulate teacher enthusiasm for using demonstrations to teach science. Robert served as a Team Leader for both the Woodrow Wilson National Fellowship Foundation and the Flinn Foundation Summer Workshop Program. Robert has received the Presidential Award, the James Bryant Conant Award in High School Teaching from the American Chemical Society, the Tandy Technology Scholar Award, a Regional Catalyst Award from the Chemical Manufacturers Association, and a Golden Apple Award from the State of Illinois.

**John G. Little** teaches chemistry and AP chemistry at St. Mary's High School in Stockton, CA. John received his B.S. and M.S. in Chemistry from University of the Pacific and has 39 years of teaching experience. Highly respected for his well-designed labs, John is the author of two lab manuals, *Chemistry Microscale Laboratory Manual* (D. C. Heath), and *Microscale Experiments for General Chemistry* (with Kenneth Williamson, Houghton Mifflin). He is also a contributing author to *Science Explorer* (Prentice Hall) and *World of Chemistry* (McDougal Littell). John served as a Chemistry Team Leader for the Woodrow Wilson National Fellowship Foundation from 1988 to 1997 and is currently a Team Leader for the Flinn Foundation Summer Workshop Program. He has been recognized for his dedicated teaching with the Tandy Technology Scholar Award and the Regional Catalyst Award from the Chemical Manufacturers Association.

**Lee Marek** retired from teaching chemistry at Naperville North High School in Naperville, IL and currently teaches at the University of Illinois–Chicago. Lee received his B.S. in Chemical Engineering from the University of Illinois and M.S. degrees in both Physics and Chemistry from Roosevelt University. He has more than 30 years of teaching experience and is currently a Team Leader for the Flinn Foundation Summer Workshop Program. His students have won national recognition in the International Chemistry Olympiad, the Westinghouse Science Talent Search, and the Internet Science and Technology Fair. Lee was also a founding member of Weird Science and has presented more than 500 demonstration and teaching workshops for more than 300,000 students and teachers across the country. Lee has performed science demonstrations on the *David Letterman Show* 20 times. Lee has received the Presidential Award, the James Bryant Conant Award in High School Teaching from the American Chemical Society, the National Catalyst Award from the Chemical Manufacturers Association, and the Tandy Technology Scholar Award.

**John Mauch** teaches chemistry and AP chemistry at Braintree High School in Braintree, MA. John received his B.A. in Chemistry from Whitworth College and M.A. in Curriculum and Education from Washington State University and has more than 25 years of teaching experience. John is an expert in microscale chemistry and is the author of two lab manuals, *Chemistry in Microscale, Volumes I and II* (Kendall/Hunt). He is also a dynamic and prolific demonstrator and workshop leader. John has presented the Flinn Scientific Chem Demo Extravaganza show at NSTA conventions for eight years and has conducted more than 100 workshops across the country. John was a Chemistry Team Member for the Woodrow Wilson National Fellowship Foundation program for four years and is currently a Board Member for the Flinn Foundation Summer Workshop Program. John has received the Massachusetts Chemistry Teacher of the Year Award from the New England Institute of Chemists.

**Dave Tanis** is Associate Professor of Chemistry at Grand Valley State University in Allendale, MI. Dave received his B.S. in Physics and Mathematics from Calvin College and M.S. in Chemistry from Case Western Reserve University. He taught high school chemistry for 26 years before joining the staff at Grand Valley State University to direct a coalition for improving pre-college math and science education. Dave later joined the faculty at Grand Valley State University and currently teaches courses for pre-service teachers. The author of two laboratory manuals, Dave acknowledges the influence of early encounters with Hubert Alyea, Marge Gardner, Henry Heikkinen, and Bassam Shakhashiri in stimulating his long-standing interest in chemical demonstrations and experiments. Continuing this tradition of mentorship, Dave has led more than 40 one-week institutes for chemistry teachers and served as a Team Member for the Woodrow Wilson National Fellowship Foundation for 13 years. He is currently a Board Member for the Flinn Foundation Summer Workshop Program. Dave received the College Science Teacher of the Year Award from the Michigan Science Teachers Association.

# Preface
## Chemical Reactions

Chemical reactions are the lifeblood of chemistry and, increasingly, of our modern world as well. The synthesis of life-saving drugs is but one example of the remarkable power of chemical reactions—the power to transform reactants into products with new and useful properties. The purpose of *Chemical Reactions,* Volume 6 in the Flinn ChemTopic™ Labs series, is to provide high school chemistry teachers with laboratory activities that will help students recognize, identify, and classify chemical reactions. A total of eleven experiments and demonstrations allow students to observe a wide variety of different chemical reactions and to develop the "chemical literacy" skills they need to be successful in chemistry.

### Observing and Classifying Reactions

Observing the properties of reactants and products is a key step in identifying chemical reactions. Some of the observations that may be associated with a chemical reaction include color changes, release of a gas, formation of a solid, and production of heat and light. All of these "signs" of a chemical reaction come together in the "Foiled Again!" demonstration, the reaction of aluminum metal with copper(II) chloride. This demonstration offers a perfect starting point for the study of chemical reactions—the observations are clues that will help students predict the products of the reaction. Observing the signs of a chemical reaction is also the starting point for "Classifying Chemical Reactions." In this experiment, students perform eight chemical reactions, identify patterns in the conversion of reactants into products, and classify the reactions into different groups. Classifying chemical reactions helps students make sense of the great variety of chemical reactions and allows them to explain what chemical reactions will occur when different substances are mixed. The demonstration "Chemical Reactions Primer" provides an alternative or supplementary activity that can be used for the same purpose. This activity features a second set of eight chemical reactions—use them to design a collaborative classroom project on chemical reactions or to assess student understanding of how reactions are classified.

### Chemical Reactions and the Principles of Chemistry

The principles and applications of chemistry reflect the principles and applications of chemical reactions! The central role of chemical reactions in the study of chemistry is examined in three experiments. In "Double Replacement Reactions and Solubility," students carry out a series of double replacement reactions, observe which combinations produce precipitates, and analyze the results to formulate general rules of solubility for ionic compounds. In "A Four-Reaction Copper Cycle," students carry out a sequence of chemical reactions that starts with copper and ends with copper. The reactions demonstrate the properties of copper and its compounds and provide additional examples of how reactions are classified. Finally, in "Chemical Reactions and Qualitative Analysis," students design and carry out a series of chemical reactions to separate and identify iron(III), silver, and zinc ions in water.

### Chemical Reaction Highlights

Recognizing chemical reactions and "translating" them into chemical equations are important skills. But chemical reactions are not formulas on a piece of paper. They are dynamic and exciting events! Some of the most exciting examples of chemical reactions have been compiled in the *Demonstrations* section of this book. There's a combination reaction that produces enough heat to fry an egg ("The Chef"), a decomposition reaction that erupts in a cascade of steaming foam ("Old Foamey"), and an oxidation reaction that gives off an eerie blue light and glows in the dark ("Cool Light"). Finally, there is an oscillating reaction that seems to defy logic and proves chemistry still has the power to surprise ("The Yellow and Blue Switcheroo").

### Safety, Flexibility, and Choice

Chemistry is an experimental science! Depend on Flinn Scientific to give you the information and confidence you need to work safely with your students and help them succeed. As your safer source for science supplies, Flinn Scientific promises you the most complete, reliable, and practical safety information for every potential lab hazard. The selection of experiments and demonstrations in *Chemical Reactions*—combined with complete sample data and extensive teacher notes—gives you the ability to design an effective lab curriculum that will work with your students and your resources in your classroom. Best of all, no matter which activities you choose, your students are assured of success. All of the activities in *Chemical Reactions* have been thoroughly tested and retested. You know they will work! Use the experiment summaries and concepts on the following pages to locate the concepts you want to teach and to choose experiments and demonstrations that will help you meet your goals.

# Format and Features

## Flinn ChemTopic™ Labs

All experiments and demonstrations in Flinn ChemTopic™ Labs are printed in a 10⅞" × 11" format with a wide 2" margin on the inside of each page. This reduces the printed area of each page to a standard 8½" × 11" format suitable for copying.

The wide margin assures you the entire printed area can be easily reproduced without damaging the binding. The margin also provides a convenient place for teachers to add their own notes.

**Concepts** — Use these bulleted lists along with state and local standards, lesson plans, and your textbook to identify activities that will allow you to accomplish specific learning goals and objectives.

**Background** — A balanced source of information for students to understand why they are doing an experiment, what they are doing, and the types of questions the activity is designed to answer. This section is not meant to be exhaustive or to replace the students' textbook, but rather to identify the core concepts that should be covered before starting the lab.

**Experiment Overview** — Clearly defines the purpose of each experiment and how students will achieve this goal. Performing an experiment without a purpose is like getting travel directions without knowing your destination. It doesn't work, especially if you run into a roadblock and need to take a detour!

**Pre-Lab Questions** — Making sure that students are prepared for lab is the single most important element of lab safety. Pre-lab questions introduce new ideas or concepts, review key calculations, and reinforce safety recommendations. The pre-lab questions may be assigned as homework in preparation for lab or they may be used as the basis of a cooperative class activity before lab.

**Materials** — Lists chemical names, formulas, and amounts for all reagents—along with specific glassware and equipment—needed to perform the experiment as written. The material dispensing area is a main source of student delay, congestion, and accidents. Three dispensing stations per room are optimum for a class of 24 students working in pairs. To safely substitute different items for any of the recommended materials, refer to the *Lab Hints* section in each experiment or demonstration.

**Safety Precautions** — Instruct and warn students of the hazards associated with the materials or procedure and give specific recommendations and precautions to protect students from these hazards. Please review this section with students before beginning each experiment.

**Procedure** — This section contains a stepwise, easy-to-follow procedure, where each step generally refers to one action item. Contains reminders about safety and recording data where appropriate. For inquiry-based experiments the procedure may restate the experiment objective and give general guidelines for accomplishing this goal.

**Data Tables** — Data tables are included for each experiment and are referred to in the procedure. These are provided for convenience and to teach students the importance of keeping their data organized in order to analyze it. To encourage more student involvement, many teachers prefer to have students prepare their own data tables. This is an excellent pre-lab preparation activity—it ensures that students have read the procedure and are prepared for lab.

**Post-Lab Questions or Data Analysis** — This section takes students step-by-step through what they did, what they observed, and what it means. Meaningful questions encourage analysis and promote critical thinking skills. Where students need to perform calculations or graph data to analyze the results, these steps are also laid out sequentially and in order.

# Format and Features

## Teacher's Notes

**Master Materials List** — Lists the chemicals, glassware, and equipment needed to perform the experiment. All amounts have been calculated for a class of 30 students working in pairs. For smaller or larger class sizes or different working group sizes, please adjust the amounts proportionately.

**Preparation of Solutions** — Calculations and procedures are given for preparing all solutions, based on a class size of 30 students working in pairs. With the exception of particularly hazardous materials, the solution amounts generally include 10% extra to account for spillage and waste. Solution volumes may be rounded to convenient glassware sizes (100-mL, 250-mL, 500-mL, etc.).

**Safety Precautions** — Repeats the safety precautions given to the students and includes more detailed information relating to safety and handling of chemicals and glassware. Refers to Material Safety Data Sheets that should be available for all chemicals used in the laboratory.

**Disposal** — Refers to the current *Flinn Scientific Catalog/Reference Manual* for general guidelines and specific procedures governing the disposal of laboratory waste. Because we recommend that teachers review local regulations before beginning any disposal procedure, the information given in this section is for general reference purposes only. However, if a disposal step is included as part of the experimental procedure itself, then the specific solutions needed for disposal are described in this section.

**Lab Hints** — This section reveals common sources of student errors and misconceptions and where students are likely to need help. Identifies the recommended length of time needed to perform each experiment, suggests alternative chemicals and equipment that may be used, and reminds teachers about new techniques (filtration, pipeting, etc.) that should be reviewed prior to lab.

**Teaching Tips** — This section puts the experiment in perspective so that teachers can judge in more detail how and where a particular experiment will fit into their curriculum. Identifies the working assumptions about what students need to know in order to perform the experiment and answer the questions. Highlights historical background and applications-oriented information that may be of interest to students.

**Sample Data** — Complete, actual sample data obtained by performing the experiment exactly as written is included for each experiment. Student data will vary.

**Answers to All Questions** — Representative or typical answers to all questions. Includes sample calculations and graphs for all data analysis questions. Information of special interest to teachers only in this section is identified by the heading "Note to the teacher." Student answers will vary.

Look for these icons in the *Experiment Summaries and Concepts* section and in the *Teacher's Notes* of individual experiments to identify inquiry-, microscale-, and technology-based experiments, respectively.

# Experiment Summaries and Concepts

## Experiment

### Classifying Chemical Reactions—Analyzing and Predicting Products

Chemists try to make sense of the great variety of chemical reactions the same way that biologists organize their knowledge of life, by sorting reactions into groups and classifying them. Classifying chemical reactions allows us to predict what chemical reactions will occur when different substances are mixed. The purpose of this experiment is to observe a variety of chemical reactions, identify patterns in the conversion of reactants into products, and classify the reactions into different groups.

### Double Replacement Reactions and Solubility—Net Ionic Equations

Precipitation reactions occur when aqueous solutions of ionic compounds are combined and a new ionic compound, which is insoluble in water, is produced. In this microscale experiment, students carry out a series of possible double replacement reactions and observe which combinations produce precipitates. Students write molecular and net ionic equations for the reactions and analyze the results to formulate general rules of solubility for ionic compounds.

### A Four-Reaction Copper Cycle—Copper and Its Compounds

How old is the copper penny in your pocket? It may be older than you think! Recovery and recycling of copper scrap is a thriving industry. In this experiment, students carry out a sequence of chemical reactions in order to demonstrate the possibilities of copper recycling. The four-reaction copper cycle demonstrates the properties of copper and its compounds, illustrates different types of chemical reactions, and provides a great test of laboratory efficiency.

### Chemical Reactions and Qualitative Analysis—An Inquiry Activity

To protect human health and safeguard the environment, the EPA regulates the amounts of barium, copper, iron, lead, silver, and zinc ions in drinking water. Qualitative analysis makes it possible to determine if these cations are present in water. In this inquiry-based experiment, students design a sequence of chemical reactions to separate and identify iron(III), silver, and zinc ions. Working out a successful qualitative analysis scheme helps students develop critical thinking and problem-solving skills.

### Chemical Reactions Primer—Observation and Classification

Chemical reactions are the lifeblood of chemistry. Recognizing chemical reactions and "translating" them into chemical equations are essential skills students need in order to be successful in chemistry. Use this activity to help your students develop "chemical literacy" skills or to assess their understanding of the five basic types of reactions.

## Concepts

- Chemical reactions
- Combination vs. decomposition
- Single vs. double replacement
- Combustion reactions

- Double replacement reactions
- Molecular equations
- Net ionic equations
- Solubility rules

- Oxidation–reduction
- Single replacement
- Double replacement
- Percent yield

- Chemical reactions
- Qualitative analysis
- Precipitation reactions
- Complex ion reactions

- Chemical reactions
- Combination vs. decomposition
- Single vs. double replacement
- Combustion reactions

# Experiment Summaries and Concepts

## Demonstration

### *Colorful Electrolysis—Decomposition of Water*

Demonstrate the electrolysis of water in simple but colorful fashion on an overhead projector using just a 9-volt battery and alligator clips. No need for expensive power supplies or fancy glassware. Color changes produced in universal indicator solution reveal the different pH conditions that develop at the anode and cathode as the decomposition reaction takes place.

### *The Chef—A Chemical Reaction that Really Cooks*

Liven up your lesson plan on chemical reactions with this fun demonstration of chemical and culinary wizardry! Would you believe the amount of heat produced when water is added to calcium oxide is enough to fry an egg? This demonstration provides an ideal introduction to chemical reactions, combination reactions, and heats of reaction.

### *Foiled Again!—Single Replacement Reaction*

Watch aluminum foil disappear when it is added to a solution of copper(II) chloride. Observe color changes, production of a gas, formation of a new solid, and a huge temperature increase. The ever-changing conditions in this demonstration of a "simple" chemical reaction will help your students practice the art and skill of laboratory observation.

### *The Yellow and Blue Switcheroo—An Oscillating Chemical Reaction*

You have spent weeks analyzing and classifying chemical reactions and your students have seen it all. Guess again! Mixing three colorless solutions generates a yellow product, which then slowly fades and changes to blue. But wait a minute—it's back to yellow again. And then back to blue! The yellow–blue color changes will continue to oscillate for about 15 minutes. If you have never performed an oscillating reaction for your students, don't pass this one up.

### *Old Foamey—Decomposition of Hydrogen Peroxide*

Bubbles and heat, foam and steam, "Old Foamey" has it all! Mix hydrogen peroxide with dishwashing liquid, add sodium iodide catalyst, then stand back and marvel as the decomposition reaction erupts in a cascade of steaming foam.

### *Cool Light—Chemiluminescence Reaction*

A wire glows, a candle burns—the production of light and heat are common to many chemical reactions. But when light is produced without heat, that's cool! Actually, it's called "cool light," and the oxidation of luminol using hydrogen peroxide provides a classic demonstration of this amazing phenomenon.

## Concepts

- Decomposition reaction
- Electrolysis
- Oxidation–reduction

- Combination reaction
- Exothermic reaction

- Single replacement reaction
- Metal activity
- Oxidation–reduction
- Catalysis

- Oscillating reactions
- Reaction mechanism

- Decomposition reaction
- Catalyst

- Chemiluminescence
- Oxidation–reduction

*Page 1 –* **Classifying Chemical Reactions**

Teacher Notes

# Classifying Chemical Reactions
## Analyzing and Predicting Products

### Introduction

The power of chemical reactions to transform our lives is visible all around us—in our homes, in our cars, even in our bodies. Chemists try to make sense of the great variety of chemical reactions the same way that biologists organize their knowledge of life, by sorting reactions into groups and classifying them. Classifying chemical reactions allows us to predict what chemical reactions will occur when different substances are mixed.

### Concepts

- Chemical reactions
- Single vs. double replacement
- Combination vs. decomposition
- Combustion reactions

### Background

A chemical reaction is defined as any process in which one or more substances are converted into new substances with different properties. Chemical reactions change the identity of the reacting substance(s) and produce new substances. Observing the properties of the reactants and products is therefore a key step in identifying chemical reactions. Some of the observations that may be associated with a chemical reaction include: (1) release of a gas; (2) formation of a precipitate; (3) color changes; (4) temperature changes; (5) emission or absorption of light. As these observations suggest, chemical reactions can be dynamic and exciting events. The essence of any chemical reaction—reactants being transformed into products—is summarized in the form of a chemical equation. Consider the reaction represented by Equation 1, the burning of natural gas (methane, $CH_4$) in a laboratory burner.

$$CH_4(g) + 2O_2(g) \rightarrow CO_2(g) + 2H_2O(g) \qquad \text{Equation 1}$$

The reactants—or, more specifically, their formulas—are written on the left side of the equation, the products on the right side of the equation. An arrow represents the direction of the reaction and is read as "yields" or "produces." Other symbols are used to describe the physical state of the reactants and products and to describe the reaction conditions (see Table 1).

Chemical reactions may be classified by considering the number of reactants and products in the reaction, the physical or chemical nature of the reactants and products, and the rearrangement of atoms in the conversion of the reactants into products (see Table 2).

*Different textbooks may classify reactions differently. Some authors treat all single replacement reactions within a much larger group of oxidation–reduction reactions. Other authors refer to double-replacement reactions as metathesis or double displacement reactions. Finally, a few authors use neither designation and classify double replacement reactions as either precipitation or acid–base reactions.*

# Classifying Chemical Reactions – Page 2

## Table 1. Symbols in Chemical Equations

| Symbol | Translation |
|---|---|
| → | Yields or produces (separates reactants from products) |
| + | Reacts with or forms alongside (separates two or more reactants or products) |
| Δ | Reaction mixture is heated (written over the arrow) |
| NR | No reaction takes place when reactants are mixed |
| (s) | Pure substance (reactant or product) is a solid |
| (l) | Pure substance (reactant or product) is a liquid |
| (g) | Pure substance (reactant or product) is a gas |
| (aq) | Aqueous solution (reactant or product is dissolved in water) |
| $\xrightarrow{Cat}$ | Catalyst—a substance needed to initiate a reaction (formula is written over the arrow) |

## Table 2. Classification of Chemical Reactions

| Type of Reaction | General Description and Example(s) |
|---|---|
| Combination | Two reactants combine to form a single product. The reactants may be elements or compounds. Also called a synthesis reaction.<br>$Zn(s) + I_2(s) \rightarrow ZnI_2(s)$<br>$CaO(s) + H_2O(l) \rightarrow Ca(OH)_2(s)$ |
| Decomposition | One reactant, a compound, breaks down to give two or more products.<br>$2H_2O_2(aq) \rightarrow 2H_2O(l) + O_2(g)$ |
| Single Replacement | An element reacts with a compound and replaces one of the elements in the compound. Metals replace hydrogen or other metals; nonmetals replace nonmetals.<br>$Zn(s) + 2HCl(aq) \rightarrow H_2(g) + ZnCl_2(aq)$<br>$Cu(s) + 2AgNO_3(aq) \rightarrow 2Ag(s) + Cu(NO_3)_2(aq)$<br>$Cl_2(aq) + 2NaI(aq) \rightarrow I_2(aq) + 2NaCl(aq)$ |
| Double Replacement | Two ionic compounds (or compounds that break apart to form ions in solution) exchange ions to form new compounds. Examples include precipitation reactions (driving force is formation of a precipitate), acid–base reactions (driving force is formation of water), and gas-forming reactions (driving force is evolution of a gas).<br>$NaCl(aq) + AgNO_3(aq) \rightarrow AgCl(s) + NaNO_3(aq)$<br>$H_2SO_4(aq) + 2NaOH(aq) \rightarrow Na_2SO_4(aq) + 2H_2O(l)$<br>$Na_2SO_3(aq) + 2HCl(aq) \rightarrow 2NaCl(aq) + H_2O(l) + SO_2(g)$ |
| Combustion | A compound burns in the presence of oxygen, producing energy in the form of heat and light. The combustion of organic compounds produces carbon dioxide and water.<br>$C_4H_8(l) + 6O_2(g) \rightarrow 4CO_2(g) + 4H_2O(g)$ |

*Page 3 – **Classifying Chemical Reactions***

Teacher Notes

### Experiment Overview

The purpose of this experiment is to observe a variety of chemical reactions and to identify patterns in the conversion of reactants into products. The properties of the reactions will be analyzed to classify the chemical reactions into different groups.

### Pre-Lab Questions

1. Which reactants used in this experiment are flammable? Discuss the safety precautions that are necessary when working with flammable materials in the lab.

2. Summarize the following description of a chemical reaction in the form of a balanced chemical equation.

    "When solid sodium bicarbonate is heated in a test tube, an invisible gas, carbon dioxide, is released into the surrounding air. Water condenses at the mouth of the test tube and a white solid residue, sodium carbonate, remains behind in the bottom of the test tube."

3. Common observations of a chemical reaction are described in the *Introduction* section. For each observation, name a common or everyday occurrence that must involve a chemical reaction. *Example:* When a candle burns, it gives off light and heat. The production of light and heat is evidence for a chemical reaction.

### Materials

| | |
|---|---|
| Ammonium carbonate, $(NH_4)_2CO_3$, 0.5 g | Butane safety lighter |
| Calcium carbonate, $CaCO_3$, 0.5 g | Evaporating dish, porcelain |
| Copper(II) chloride solution, $CuCl_2$, 0.5 M, 4 mL | Forceps or crucible tongs |
| Ethyl alcohol, $C_2H_5OH$, 1 mL | Heat-resistant pad |
| Hydrochloric acid, HCl, 1 M, 4 mL | Litmus paper |
| Magnesium ribbon, Mg, 2–4 cm strips, 2 | Pipets, Beral-type, 6 |
| Phenolphthalein indicator, 1 drop | Spatula |
| Sodium hydroxide solution, NaOH, 1 M, 1 mL | Test tubes, small, 6 |
| Sodium phosphate solution, $Na_3PO_4$, 0.5 M, 1 mL | Test tube clamp |
| Water, distilled | Test tube rack |
| Zinc, mossy, or zinc shot, Zn, 1–2 pieces | Wash bottle |
| Bunsen or laboratory burner | Wood splints, 3 |

### Safety Precautions

*Ethyl alcohol is a flammable solvent and a dangerous fire risk. Keep away from flames and other sources of ignition. Solvent bottles should be kept capped at all times and must be removed from the work area when using the laboratory burner. Addition of denaturant makes ethyl alcohol poisonous. Hydrochloric acid and sodium hydroxide solutions are corrosive liquids. Notify the teacher and clean up all spills immediately. Phenolphthalein is an alcohol-based solution and is flammable; it is moderately toxic by ingestion. Magnesium metal is a flammable solid and zinc metal may contain flammable dust. Copper(II) chloride solution is toxic by ingestion. Avoid contact of all chemicals with eyes and skin. Wear chemical splash goggles and chemical-resistant gloves and apron. Wash hands thoroughly with soap and water before leaving the lab.*

---

*See the* Lab Hints *section for recommendations that will help make this lab run more smoothly. For best results, set up eight stations around the room for the eight different reactions. At each station, place all of the reagents and equipment that students will need to run that reaction. Two groups of students should be able to work comfortably at each station.*

# Classifying Chemical Reactions – Page 4

## Procedure

Teacher Notes

For each reaction, record the color and appearance of the reactant(s), the evidence for a chemical reaction, and the properties of the product(s) in the data table.

### Reaction #1

1. Obtain a 3–4 cm strip of magnesium metal ribbon. Hold the piece of magnesium with forceps or crucible tongs and heat the metal in a laboratory burner flame. *Caution:* Do not look directly at the burning magnesium—ultraviolet light that is produced may damage your eyes.

2. When the magnesium ignites, remove it from the flame and hold it over an evaporating dish or a Pyrex® watch glass until the metal has burned completely. Let the product fall into the evaporating dish.

3. Turn off the laboratory burner and observe the properties of the product in the evaporating dish.

4. Record observations in the data table.

### Reaction #2

5. Using a Beral-type pipet, add about 2 mL (40 drops) of 1 M hydrochloric acid solution to a small test tube.

6. Obtain a 2–3 cm strip of magnesium metal ribbon and coil it loosely into a small ball. Add the magnesium metal to the acid in the test tube.

7. Carefully feel the sides of the test tube and observe the resulting chemical reaction for about 30 seconds.

8. While the reaction is still occuring, light a wood splint and quickly place the burning splint in the mouth of the test tube. Do not put the burning splint into the acid solution.

9. Record observations in the data table.

### Reaction #3

10. Obtain a clean and dry test tube and place a small amount (about the size of a jelly bean) of ammonium carbonate into the test tube.

11. Use a test tube clamp to hold the test tube and gently heat the tube in a laboratory burner flame for about 30 seconds.

12. Remove the test tube from the flame and place a piece of moistened litmus paper in the mouth of the test tube. Identify any odor that is readily apparent by wafting the fumes toward your nose. *Caution:* Do NOT sniff the test tube!

13. Test for the formation of a gas: Light a wood splint and insert the burning splint halfway down into the test tube.

14. Record observations in the data table.

*See the* Supplementary Information *section for a description of the burning and glowing splint tests. The teacher may wish to demonstrate a control test for comparison—when a burning splint is inserted into an empty (air-filled) test tube, nothing happens.*

Flinn ChemTopic™ Labs — Chemical Reactions

*Teacher Notes*

### Reaction #4

15. Place a small amount (about the size of a jelly bean) of calcium carbonate in a clean and dry test tube.

16. Using a Beral-type pipet, add about 1 mL (20 drops) of 1 M hydrochloric acid to the test tube. Feel the sides of the test tube and observe the reaction for 30 seconds.

17. Quickly light a wood splint and insert the burning splint about halfway down into the test tube. Do not allow the burning splint to contact the reaction mixture.

18. Record observations in the data table.

### Reactions #5

19. Using a Beral-type pipet, add about 2 mL (40 drops) of 0.5 M copper(II) chloride solution into a small test tube.

20. Add 1–2 pieces of mossy zinc or one piece of zinc shot to the test tube and observe the resulting chemical reaction.

21. Record observations in the data table.

### Reaction #6

22. Using a Beral-type pipet, add about 2 mL (40 drops) of 0.5 M copper(II) chloride solution into a small test tube.

23. Using a fresh pipet, add about 25 drops of 0.5 M sodium phosphate solution to the test tube.

24. Record observations in the data table.

### Reaction #7

25. Using a Beral-type pipet, add 20 drops of 1 M sodium hydroxide solution into a small test tube.

26. Add one drop of phenolphthalein indicator to the test tube and mix the solution by gently swirling the tube. *Hint:* Phenolphthalein is called an "acid–base" indicator.

27. Using a clean Beral-type pipet, add 1 M hydrochloric acid solution one drop at a time to the test tube. Count the number of drops of acid required for a permanent color change to be observed.

28. Record observations in the data table.

*For convenience, have students mark the 2-mL level on each test tube.*

# Classifying Chemical Reactions – Page 6

### Reaction #8

29. Working in the hood or a designated work area, add about 1 mL (20 drops) of ethyl alcohol to a clean evaporating dish. Place the evaporating dish on a heat-resistant pad.

30. Cap the alcohol bottle and remove it from the work area.

31. Fill a test tube about one-third full with cold tap water for use in step 34.

32. Light a butane safety lighter and bring the flame close to the alcohol in the evaporating dish.

33. Turn off the safety lighter as soon as the alcohol ignites.

34. Place the test tube containing cold water in a test tube clamp and hold the test tube above the burning alcohol. Observe the outside of the test tube for evidence of product formation.

35. Allow the alcohol to burn until it is completely consumed. *Caution:* Do not touch the hot evaporating dish.

36. Record observations in the data table.

---

**Teacher Notes**

*Do not do Reaction #8 unless a designated work area for ethyl alcohol can be set up in an isolated location. For a safer, alternative example of combustion, simply set up a 250-mL beaker with cold water on a ring stand over a laboratory burner. Light the burner and immediately observe water condensing on the outside of the beaker.*

Teacher Notes

Name: _____

Class/Lab Period: _____

# Classifying Chemical Reactions

**Data Table**

| Reaction | Appearance of Reactant(s), Evidence of Chemical Reaction, and Properties of Product(s) |
|---|---|
| 1 | |
| 2 | |
| 3 | |
| 4 | |
| 5 | |
| 6 | |
| 7 | |
| 8 | |

# Classifying Chemical Reactions – *Page 8*

**Post-Lab Questions**  *Teacher Notes*

1. Write a balanced chemical equation for each reaction #1–8. Classify each reaction using the information provided in the *Background* section (see Table 2).

   Reaction #1:

   Reaction #2:

   Reaction #3:

   Reaction #4:

   Reaction #5:

   Reaction #6:

   Reaction #7:

   Reaction #8:

2. Classifying chemical reactions helps chemists to predict the possible products that will form when two or more substances are mixed. Complete and balance the following equations by predicting the products of each chemical reaction.

   (a) Double replacement: $NaOH(aq) + CuSO_4(aq) \rightarrow$

   (b) Combination: $Al(s) + O_2(g) \rightarrow$

   (c) Combustion: $C_6H_{12}O_6(s) + O_2(g) \rightarrow$

   (d) Decomposition: $CaCO_3(s) \xrightarrow{\Delta}$

   (e) Single replacement: $Fe(s) + Pb(NO_3)_2(aq) \rightarrow$

3. *(Optional)* Complete the "Classifying Chemical Reactions Worksheet."

*Question #1 is the most difficult task in this experiment. Cooperative learning groups may help students "translate" their observations in the form of a chemical equation. Have students look at the formulas of the reactants (see the Materials section) for clues concerning the identity of possible products.*

Flinn ChemTopic™ Labs — Chemical Reactions

**Teacher Notes**

Name: _____

Class/Lab Period: _____

# Classifying Chemical Reactions Worksheet

Write a balanced chemical equation for each reaction and classify the reaction.

1. Copper metal heated with oxygen gives solid copper(II) oxide.

2. Mixing ammonium nitrate and sodium hydroxide solutions gives aqueous sodium nitrate, ammonia gas, and water.

3. Mercury(II) nitrate solution reacts with potassium iodide solution to give a mercury(II) iodide precipitate and potassium nitrate solution.

4. Aluminum metal and sulfuric acid yield aqueous aluminum sulfate and hydrogen gas.

5. Acetic acid and lithium hydroxide solution produce water and aqueous lithium acetate.

6. Sulfur dioxide gas reacts with oxygen on a platinum catalyst surface to produce sulfur trioxide gas.

7. Sodium metal reacts with water to give sodium hydroxide solution and hydrogen gas.

8. Heating solid nickel chloride dihydrate yields solid nickel chloride and water vapor.

9. Heating solid potassium chlorate in the presence of manganese dioxide catalyst produces potassium chloride and oxygen gas.

*This optional worksheet may be used as a review sheet or for post-lab assessment.*

# Teacher's Notes
## Classifying Chemical Reactions

### Master Materials List *(for a class of 30 students working in pairs)*

Ammonium carbonate, $(NH_4)_2CO_3$, 7–10 g
Calcium carbonate, $CaCO_3$, 7–10 g
Copper(II) chloride solution, $CuCl_2$, 0.5 M, 75 mL
Ethyl alcohol, $C_2H_5OH$, 25 mL
Hydrochloric acid, HCl, 1 M, 75 mL
Magnesium ribbon, 2–4 cm strips, 30
Phenolphthalein indicator, 0.5%, 5 mL
Sodium hydroxide solution, NaOH, 1 M, 25 mL
Sodium phosphate solution, $Na_3PO_4$, 0.5 M, 25 mL
Water, distilled or deionized
Zinc, mossy, Zn, 30–50 pieces
Bunsen burners, 15
Butane safety lighters, 3–5
Evaporating dishes, 15
Forceps or crucible tongs, 15
Heat-resistant pads, 15
Litmus paper, 15 strips
Pipets, Beral-type, 90
Spatulas, 15
Test tubes, small, 90
Test tube clamps, 15
Test tube racks, 15
Wash bottles, 15
Wood splints, 45

### Preparation of Solutions *(for a class of 30 students working in pairs)*

*Copper(II) Chloride, 0.5 M:* Dissolve 8.5 g of copper(II) chloride dihydrate ($CuCl_2 \cdot 2H_2O$) in about 50 mL of distilled or deionized water. Stir to dissolve and dilute to 100 mL with water.

*Hydrochloric Acid, 1 M:* Place about 25 mL of distilled or deionized water in a graduated cylinder or volumetric flask and add 8.3 mL of concentrated (12.1 M) hydrochloric acid. Stir to mix and then dilute to 100 mL with water. *Note:* Always add acid to water.

*Sodium Hydroxide, 1 M:* Cool about 25 mL of distilled or deionized water in an ice-water bath and add 2.0 g of fresh sodium hydroxide pellets. Stir to dissolve and then dilute to 50 mL with water.

*Sodium Phosphate, 0.5 M:* Dissolve 9.5 g of sodium phosphate dodecahydrate ($Na_3PO_4 \cdot 12H_2O$) in 50 mL of distilled or deionized water.

### Safety Precautions

*Ethyl alcohol is a flammable solvent and a dangerous fire risk. Keep away from flames and other sources of ignition. Solvent bottles should be kept capped at all times and must be removed from the work area when using the laboratory burner. Addition of denaturant makes ethyl alcohol poisonous. Hydrochloric acid and sodium hydroxide solutions are corrosive liquids. Keep sodium carbonate and citric acid on hand to clean up acid and base spills, respectively. Phenolphthalein is an alcohol-based solution and is flammable; it is moderately toxic by ingestion. Magnesium metal is a flammable solid and zinc metal may contain a flammable dust. Copper(II) chloride solution is highly toxic by ingestion. Avoid contact of all chemicals with eyes and skin. Wear chemical splash goggles and chemical-resistant gloves and apron. Please consult current Material Safety Data Sheets for additional safety, handling, and disposal information. Remind students to wash their hands thoroughly with soap and water before leaving the lab.*

Butane safety lighters are available from Flinn Scientific (Catalog No. AP8960). They may also be purchased at hardware stores (they are sold as barbeque lighters). Do not use cigarette lighters.

# Teacher's Notes

**Teacher Notes** (handwritten):

Gas Tests for

H₂ – pop
CO₂ – extinguish & limewater
NH₃ – odor, litmus
O₂ – glowing splint

Litmus and Phenolphthalein

Tell Kids

#2. – put burning splint into gas
– exothermic rxn

#3. H₂O(g) is an additional product

#7. stir as you add drops

#8. ethanol = ethyl alcohol

use burning splint (not butane safety lighter)

## Disposal

Consult your current *Flinn Scientific Catalog/Reference Manual* for general guidelines and specific procedures governing the disposal of laboratory waste. Excess sodium hydroxide solution may be neutralized with acid and disposed of according to Flinn Suggested Disposal Method #10. Excess hydrochloric acid may be neutralized with base and disposed of according to Flinn Suggested Disposal Method #24b. The mixture resulting from Reaction #5 contains solid copper metal which will clog the drains if discarded in the sink. Pour this mixture onto a pair of thickly folded paper towels and discard in the trash according to Flinn Suggested Disposal Method #26a. All other reaction mixtures may be washed down the drain with plenty of excess water according to Flinn Suggested Disposal Method #26b.

## Lab Hints

- The goal of this survey experiment is for students to develop "chemical literacy" skills by observing as many chemical reactions as is practical. The laboratory work for this experiment can easily be completed within a typical 50-minute lab period. For best results, have students complete the *Pre-Lab Questions* the day before lab. This will help ensure that students are prepared for lab and understand the safety precautions. Student preparation is an essential element of lab safety.

- To ease congestion and improve efficiency in the lab, set up eight stations around the lab, one station per reaction. Students may rotate through the stations in any order. "Down time" between stations may be used to record observations.

- Additional reactions may be assigned, if desired, to give students more experience recognizing and interpreting chemical reactions. See the "Chemical Reactions Primer" in the *Demonstrations* section of this book for a second set of eight reactions that may be used as an alternative procedure or as part of a collaborative classroom activity.

- For safety reasons, we recommend using porcelain evaporating dishes to test the flammability of ethyl alcohol. If glass evaporating dishes or watch glasses are substituted instead, check the glassware for cracks and chips, and make sure all glassware is made from heat-resistant borosilicate (e.g., Pyrex®) glass.

- Students may not be familiar with the properties of the common gases that are used to identify the gaseous products in reactions #2, 3, and 4. See the "Properties and Identification of Common Gases" in the *Supplementary Information* section for a convenient summary and student handout.

## Teaching Tips

- This experiment provides experience in recognizing chemical reactions, writing chemical equations, and classifying chemical reactions. The best time to do this experiment is prior to lecture instruction on the topic. Students who get the theory before the practice tend to think of chemical reactions as formulas on a piece of paper. As discussed in the *Background* section, chemical reactions are quite showy events, with lots of interesting observations. In most cases, the observations themselves will enable students to identify or predict the products from the known structures of the reactants.

# Teacher's Notes

- See the *Demonstrations* section in this lab manual for popular demonstrations of other chemical reactions. "The Chef" shows the highly exothermic combination reaction of calcium oxide and water, while "Electrolysis of Water" illustrates the decomposition reaction of water. "Foiled Again" demonstrates the single replacement reaction of aluminum with copper(II) chloride and is a wonderful activity to use to develop students' observation skills.

- Two types of reaction are so important in chemistry that we have devoted entire books in the *Flinn ChemTopic™ Labs* series to them. See "Acids and Bases," Volume 13 in the series, and "Oxidation–Reduction," Volume 16 in the series.

## Answers to Pre-Lab Questions *(Student answers will vary.)*

1. Which reactants used in this experiment are flammable? Discuss the safety precautions that are necessary when working with flammable materials in the lab.

   *Ethyl alcohol is a flammable solvent. Keep away from flames and other sources of ignition. Cap the solvent bottle and remove it, along with all other flammable materials, from the designated work area when doing the burning alcohol test.*

2. Summarize the following description of a chemical reaction in the form of a balanced chemical equation.

   "When solid sodium bicarbonate is heated in a test tube, an invisible gas, carbon dioxide, is released into the surrounding air. Water condenses at the mouth of the test tube and a white solid residue, sodium carbonate, remains behind in the bottom of the test tube."

   $2NaHCO_3(s) \xrightarrow{\Delta} Na_2CO_3(s) + H_2O(l) + CO_2(g)$

3. Common observations of a chemical reaction are described in the *Introduction* section. For each observation, name a common or everyday occurrence that must involve a chemical reaction. *Example:* When a candle burns, it gives off light and heat. The production of light and heat is evidence for a chemical reaction.

| Sign of Reaction | Example(s) |
| --- | --- |
| Release of gas | *Alka-Seltzer® dissolving in water* <br> *Combining baking soda and vinegar* |
| Precipitate formation | *Hard water (scale) deposits in bathroom* <br> *Milk curdles when it turns sour* |
| Color changes | *Corrosion of iron* <br> *Adding lemon juice to tea* |
| Temperature changes | *Burning natural gas in a stove or furnace* <br> *"Burning" glucose in our bodies* |
| Light absorption or emission | *Photosynthesis in green plants* <br> *A firefly glows at night (bioluminescence)* |

# Teacher's Notes

## Sample Data

*Student data will vary.*

### Data Table

| Reaction | Appearance of Reactant(s), Evidence of Chemical Reaction, and Properties of Product(s) |
|---|---|
| 1 | Magnesium metal ribbon is silver and shiny. When placed in a flame, it burns slowly with a yellow flame. It then bursts into an intense, bright white flame. The product of the reaction is a dull, grayish-white powder that crumbles easily. |
| 2 | Rapid bubbling occurs when magnesium is added to the acid solution. The test tube feels warm. When a burning wood splint is placed in the mouth of the test tube, a large "pop" is heard, the flame goes out, and condensation is then seen on the inside of the test tube. The final solution is clear and colorless. |
| 3 | Ammonium carbonate is a white solid with a strong ammonia odor. Heating releases more ammonia. Moistened litmus paper turns blue when exposed to the ammonia vapor. Burning splint is extinguished by invisible gas inside the test tube. A clear liquid condenses at the mouth of the test tube. |
| 4 | Adding hydrochloric acid to solid calcium carbonate produces vigorous bubbling. The reaction is instantaneous and is over in less than a minute. When a burning wood splint is placed in the test tube, the flame is extinguished. The products are a gas and a clear solution. |
| 5 | The mossy zinc is shiny gray and turns dark when added to copper(II) chloride solution. The color of the solution changes from blue to greenish blue and then pale gray. The zinc acquires a spongy, dark red coating, which builds up quickly and then crumbles or flakes off. The test tube feels hot. Final solution is pale gray, almost colorless. |
| 6 | The copper(II) chloride solution is blue-green. Adding a colorless solution of sodium phosphate produces a bulky turquoise precipitate. The initial blue color of the solution fades and the final products consist of a turquoise solid and a pale blue liquid. |
| 7 | Sodium hydroxide solution is colorless but turns bright pink when phenolphthalein is added. The color of the solution changes back to colorless after 21–22 drops of hydrochloric acid have been added. The test tube feels slightly warm to the touch. |
| 8 | Ethyl alcohol is a clear and colorless liquid. It quickly catches on fire when exposed to a flame. The burning alcohol flame is blue (yellow at the tips). It takes less than a minute for the alcohol to burn completely. The air above the burning liquid is hot. A clear liquid condenses on the outside of the cold test tube passed over the flame. |

# Teacher's Notes

**Answers to Post-Lab Questions** *(Student answers will vary.)*

1. Write a balanced chemical equation for each reaction #1–8. Classify each reaction using the information provided in the Background section (see Table 2).

   Reaction #1:    $2Mg(s) + O_2(g) \rightarrow 2MgO(s)$
   Combination

   Reaction #2:    $Mg(s) + 2HCl(aq) \rightarrow MgCl_2(aq) + H_2(g)$
   Single replacement

   Reaction #3:    $(NH_4)_2CO_3(s) \xrightarrow{\Delta} 2NH_3(g) + CO_2(g) + H_2O(l)$
   Decomposition

   Reaction #4:    $CaCO_3(s) + 2HCl(aq) \rightarrow CaCl_2(aq) + H_2O(l) + CO_2(g)$
   Double replacement

   Reaction #5:    $Zn(s) + CuCl_2(aq) \rightarrow Cu(s) + ZnCl_2(aq)$
   Single replacement

   Reaction #6:    $3CuCl_2(aq) + 2Na_3PO_4(aq) \rightarrow Cu_3(PO_4)_2(s) + 6NaCl(aq)$
   Double replacement

   Reaction #7:    $HCl(aq) + NaOH(aq) \rightarrow NaCl(aq) + H_2O(l)$
   Double replacement

   Reaction #8:    $C_2H_6O(l) + 3O_2(g) \rightarrow 2CO_2(g) + 3H_2O(g)$
   Combustion

2. Classifying chemical reactions helps chemists to predict the possible products that will form when two or more substances are mixed. Complete and balance the following equations by predicting the products of each chemical reaction.

   (a) Double replacement: $2NaOH(aq) + CuSO_4(aq) \rightarrow Cu(OH)_2(s) + Na_2SO_4(aq)$

   (b) Combination: $4Al(s) + 3O_2(g) \rightarrow 2Al_2O_3(s)$

   (c) Combustion: $C_6H_{12}O_6(s) + 6O_2(g) \rightarrow 6CO_2(g) + 6H_2O(l)$

   (d) Decomposition: $CaCO_3(s) \rightarrow CaO(s) + CO_2(g)$

   (e) Single replacement: $2Fe(s) + 3Pb(NO_3)_2(aq) \rightarrow 3Pb(s) + 2Fe(NO_3)_3(aq)$

3. *(Optional)* Complete the "Classifying Chemical Reactions Worksheet."

---

Teacher Notes

*Students will be confused about the double-replacement label for Reaction #4. It may help to write out the overall reaction in two steps—formation of carbonic acid ($H_2CO_3$) followed by decomposition to give water and carbon dioxide.*

Teacher Notes

# Classifying Chemical Reactions Worksheet
## Answer Key

Write a balanced chemical equation for each reaction and classify the reaction.

1. Copper metal heated with oxygen gives solid copper(II) oxide.

    $2Cu(s) + O_2(g) \xrightarrow{\Delta} 2CuO(s)$      *Combination*

2. Mixing ammonium nitrate and sodium hydroxide solutions gives aqueous sodium nitrate, ammonia gas, and water.

    $NH_4NO_3(aq) + NaOH(aq) \rightarrow NaNO_3(aq) + NH_3(g) + H_2O(l)$      *Double replacement*

3. Mercury(II) nitrate solution reacts with potassium iodide solution to give a mercury(II) iodide precipitate and potassium nitrate solution.

    $Hg(NO_3)_2(aq) + 2KI(aq) \rightarrow HgI_2(s) + 2KNO_3(aq)$      *Double replacement*

4. Aluminum metal and sulfuric acid yield aqueous aluminum sulfate and hydrogen gas.

    $2Al(s) + 3H_2SO_4(aq) \rightarrow Al_2(SO_4)_3(aq) + 3H_2(g)$      *Single replacement*

5. Acetic acid and lithium hydroxide solution produce water and aqueous lithium acetate.

    $HC_2H_3O_2(aq) + LiOH(aq) \rightarrow H_2O(l) + LiC_2H_3O_2(aq)$      *Double replacement*

6. Sulfur dioxide gas reacts with oxygen on a platinum catalyst surface to produce sulfur trioxide gas.

    $2SO_2(g) + O_2(g) \xrightarrow{Pt} 2SO_3(g)$      *Combination*

7. Sodium metal reacts with water to give sodium hydroxide solution and hydrogen gas.

    $2Na(s) + 2H_2O(l) \rightarrow 2NaOH(aq) + H_2(g)$      *Single replacement*

8. Heating solid nickel chloride dihydrate yields solid nickel chloride and water vapor.

    $NiCl_2 \cdot 2H_2O(s) \xrightarrow{\Delta} NiCl_2(s) + 2H_2O(g)$      *Decomposition (dehydration)*

9. Heating solid potassium chlorate in the presence of manganese dioxide catalyst produces potassium chloride and oxygen gas.

    $2KClO_3(s) \xrightarrow{MnO_2} 2KCl(s) + 3O_2(g)$      *Decomposition*

# Teacher's Notes

## Supplementary Information

### Properties and Identification of Common Gases

Many common gases can be identified by testing their combustion properties (the burning splint test) and/or their acid–base properties (the litmus test).

Carbon dioxide gas ($CO_2$) is more dense than air and does not support combustion. If a burning wood splint is inserted into a container of carbon dioxide, the flame will be smothered or extinguished due to the lack of oxygen. Carbon dioxide gas dissolves in water to give an acidic solution, and can be detected using a saturated limewater solution, $Ca(OH)_2(aq)$. Carbon dioxide combines with calcium hydroxide to form calcium carbonate, which precipitates from solution.

$$CO_2(g) + H_2O(l) \rightleftharpoons H_2CO_3(aq)$$

$$H_2CO_3(aq) \rightleftharpoons H^+(aq) + HCO_3^-(aq)$$

$$CO_2(g) + Ca(OH)_2(aq) \rightarrow CaCO_3(s) + H_2O(l)$$

Oxygen gas ($O_2$) supports combustion and is necessary for combustion reactions to occur. If a glowing (not burning) splint is placed in an oxygen atmosphere, it will reignite and burn brightly.

Hydrogen gas ($H_2$) is less dense than air and is flammable. It forms an explosive mixture with air. When a burning splint is exposed to hydrogen gas, a loud "pop" is usually heard as the hydrogen explodes and the flame is extinguished. The product of the combustion reaction of hydrogen is water. Hydrogen is essentially insoluble in water.

$$2H_2(g) + O_2(g) \rightarrow 2H_2O(l)$$

Ammonia gas ($NH_3$) has a characteristic odor and dissolves readily in water to give a basic solution. Ammonia can be detected by placing a piece of moist litmus paper in the stream of ammonia gas released from a reaction mixture. The litmus paper turns blue (basic) due to the formation of hydroxide ions, as shown below.

$$NH_3(aq) + H_2O(l) \rightleftharpoons NH_4^+(aq) + OH^-(aq)$$

Sulfur dioxide ($SO_2$) and sulfur trioxide ($SO_3$) are colorless gases with a stinging odor. They dissolve in water to form acidic solutions.

$$SO_2(g) + H_2O(l) \rightleftharpoons H^+(aq) + HSO_3^-(aq)$$

$$SO_3(g) + H_2O(l) \rightleftharpoons H^+(aq) + HSO_4^-(aq)$$

---

Teacher Notes

*Use this as a supplementary handout to help students identify products and write chemical equations.*

*Teacher Notes*

# Double Replacement Reactions and Solubility
## Net Ionic Equations

### Introduction

Precipitation reactions, a type of double replacement reaction, are widely used to prepare new compounds and analyze their purity. Precipitation reactions occur when aqueous solutions of ionic compounds are combined and a new ionic compound, which is insoluble in water, is produced. The result is the formation of a precipitate, a solid which settles out of the solution. By carrying out a series of possible double replacement reactions and observing which combinations produce precipitates, we should be able to determine some general rules of solubility for ionic compounds in water.

### Concepts

- Double replacement reactions
- Net ionic equations
- Molecular equations
- Solubility rules

### Background

*Double replacement reactions* occur when two ionic compounds (or compounds that break apart to form ions in aqueous solution) exchange ions to form new compounds. Double replacement reactions generally occur in one direction only in response to a "driving force," which provides a reason for the reaction to occur. Two important driving forces for reactions between ions in aqueous solution are formation of a solid (precipitation reactions) and formation of a gas or stable molecular product (acid–base neutralization reactions). In the absence of a driving force, ionic compounds will remain dissolved in solution and no chemical reaction will take place among the dissolved ions.

When an ionic compound dissolves in water, the crystalline solid dissociates or separates into its corresponding cations and anions. For example, silver nitrate dissociates into silver cations and nitrate anions (Equation 1).

$$AgNO_3(s) \rightarrow Ag^+(aq) + NO_3^-(aq) \qquad \text{Equation 1}$$

When solutions containing two ionic compounds are mixed, two new combinations of cations and anions are possible. In some cases, the cation from one compound and the anion from the other compound may combine to form an insoluble product, which is called a precipitate. For example, when sodium bromide is added to a solution of silver nitrate, there are four different ions present and two new combinations of cations and anions—sodium nitrate and silver bromide—are possible. Sodium nitrate is soluble in water and its ions remain dissolved in solution. Silver bromide is insoluble in water and precipitates from solution as a solid (Equation 2).

$$AgNO_3(aq) + NaBr(aq) \rightarrow AgBr(s) + NaNO_3(aq) \qquad \text{Equation 2}$$

---

*All chemical reactions need some reason for taking place. The driving force for a reaction is best described thermodynamically in terms of ΔG, the free energy change for the reaction. The free energy, in turn, reflects a competitive balance between two more fundamental forces in nature—the tendency to decrease (lose) energy and the tendency to increase entropy. The driving forces identified in the* Background *section represent "clues" that can be used to predict if a reaction will occur.*

# Double Replacement Reactions and Solubility – Page 2

Equation 2 summarizes the double replacement reaction between silver nitrate and sodium bromide. It is called a *molecular equation* because the reactants and products are represented by their molecular formulas. The actual reaction process can be better understood if we rewrite the equation to represent the ionic compounds as they exist in solution, that is, in the form of their dissolved ions.

The *complete ionic equation* for the double replacement reaction of silver nitrate and sodium bromide is shown in Equation 3. Because silver bromide is not soluble, it is best represented by its formula, AgBr.

$$Ag^+(aq) + NO_3^-(aq) + Na^+(aq) + Br^-(aq) \rightarrow$$
$$AgBr(s) + Na^+(aq) + NO_3^-(aq) \qquad \textit{Equation 3}$$

Notice that some ions (Na$^+$ and NO$_3^-$) appear on both sides of the equation in Equation 3. These ions are referred to as *spectator ions* because they do not participate in the overall reaction. Just as in algebra, where a term that appears on both sides of an equation may be "cancelled out," we can do the same thing with the complete ionic equation shown in Equation 3. Subtracting the spectator ions from both sides gives the *net ionic equation* for the precipitation reaction of silver bromide (Equation 4).

$$Ag^+(aq) + Br^-(aq) \rightarrow AgBr(s) \qquad \textit{Equation 4}$$

Double replacement reactions may be used to determine some general *solubility rules* for ionic compounds in water. If a precipitation reaction occurs when solutions of ionic compounds are mixed, then at least one of the two possible products formed by the "ion exchange" reaction must be insoluble in water. In this experiment, various ionic solutions will be mixed two at a time to determine which combinations will form precipitates. Knowing the ions that are present will make it possible to predict the solubility pattern of different ionic compounds.

## Experiment Overview

The purpose of this experiment is to carry out a series of possible double replacement reactions and analyze the results to formulate some general rules of solubility for ionic compounds. The solutions that will be mixed fall into two categories. The "anion testing solutions" contain sodium salts with six different anions (sodium carbonate, sodium chloride, sodium hydroxide, etc.), while the "cation testing solutions" contain nitrate salts with eight different cations (aluminum nitrate, barium nitrate, calcium nitrate, etc.) All sodium salts and all nitrate salts are soluble in water—therefore, any precipitate that is observed when an anion and cation testing solution are combined should be easy to identify.

*Page 3* – **Double Replacement Reactions and Solubility**

Teacher Notes

**Pre-Lab Questions**

1. Read the entire *Procedure,* including the *Safety Precautions*. Which solutions used in this experiment are described as skin and eye irritants? What does this mean? What precautions are used to protect against these hazards?

2. Solutions of calcium, zinc, and lead nitrate were mixed pairwise with sodium iodide, sodium sulfate, and sodium chromate using the procedure described in this experiment (see the following table of results). Write a molecular equation and a net ionic equation for each double replacement reaction that produced a precipitate.

|  | Calcium Nitrate, $Ca(NO_3)_2$ | Lead Nitrate, $Pb(NO_3)_2$ | Zinc Nitrate, $Zn(NO_3)_2$ |
| --- | --- | --- | --- |
| Sodium Chromate, $Na_2CrO_4$ | PPT | PPT | PPT |
| Sodium Iodide, NaI | NR | PPT | NR |
| Sodium Sulfide, $Na_2S$ | NR | PPT | PPT |

3. What are the advantages and disadvantages of using molecular equations, complete ionic equations, and net ionic equations to describe double replacement reactions?

**Materials**

*Anion Testing Solutions, 0.1 M*
Sodium carbonate, $Na_2CO_3$, 3 mL
Sodium chloride, NaCl, 3 mL
Sodium hydroxide, NaOH, 3 mL
Sodium iodide, NaI, 3 mL
Sodium phosphate, $Na_3PO_4$, 3 mL
Sodium sulfate, $Na_2SO_4$, 3 mL

*Cation Testing Solutions, 0.1 M*
Aluminum nitrate, $Al(NO_3)_3$, 2 mL
Ammonium nitrate, $NH_4NO_3$, 2 mL
Barium nitrate, $Ba(NO_3)_2$, 2 mL
Calcium nitrate, $Ca(NO_3)_2$, 2 mL
Copper(II) nitrate, $Cu(NO_3)_2$, 2 mL
Iron(III) nitrate, $Fe(NO_3)_3$, 2 mL
Silver nitrate, $AgNO_3$, 2 mL
Zinc nitrate, $Zn(NO_3)_2$, 2 mL

*Equipment*
Cotton swabs
Distilled water and wash bottle
Labels, adhesive, 14
Paper towels

Pipets, thin stem, 14
Pipet holder (24-well plate)
Reaction plate, 96-well
Toothpicks

**Safety Precautions**

*Ammonium nitrate, barium nitrate, copper(II) nitrate, and silver nitrate solutions are slightly toxic by ingestion. Silver nitrate, sodium carbonate, and sodium hydroxide solutions are skin and eye irritants; silver nitrate will also stain skin and clothing. Avoid contact of all chemicals with eyes and skin. Wear chemical splash goggles and chemical-resistant gloves and apron. Wash hands thoroughly with soap and water before leaving the lab.*

# Double Replacement Reactions and Solubility – Page 4

## Procedure

### Preparation

*Steps 1–4 may only need to be done once by the first class section doing the experiment.*

1. Obtain 14 thin stem pipets and 14 blank labels. Using a permanent marker or wax pencil, write the names of the 14 solutions listed in the *Materials* section on the labels. Write on only one-half of each label—the labels will be folded in half around the pipets.

2. Fold the labels in half around the pipet stems just above the bulbs, as shown in Figure 1a.

3. Cut the stem of each pipet at a 45° angle about 5 cm from the bulb (Figure 1a). The shorter stems will make it easier to deliver uniform-size drops.

4. Fill each pipet with the appropriate solution and store the filled pipets stem-side-up in the 24-well plate, as shown in Figure 1b.

5. Place a clean 96-well reaction plate on top of a sheet of black paper as shown below. Each well is identified by a unique combination of a letter and a number—horizontal rows are identified by the letters A–H and vertical columns are numbered from 1 to 12 (Figure 2).

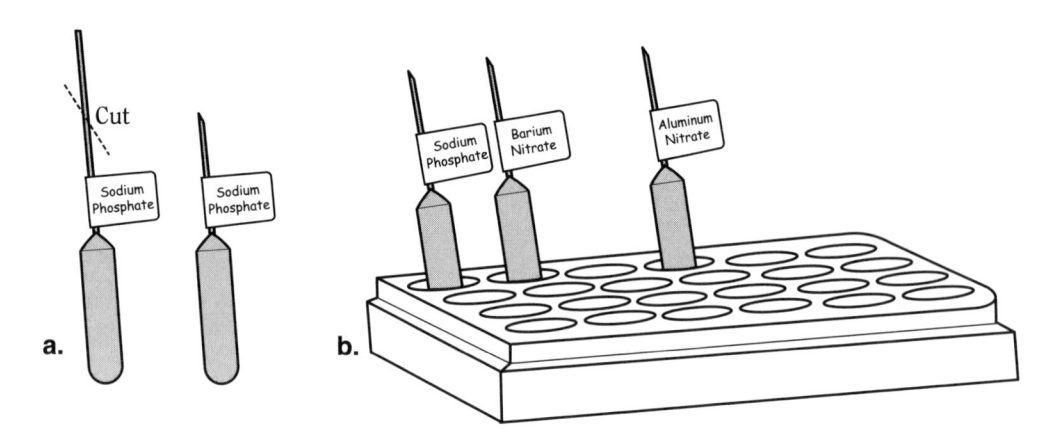

**Figures 1a and 1b.**

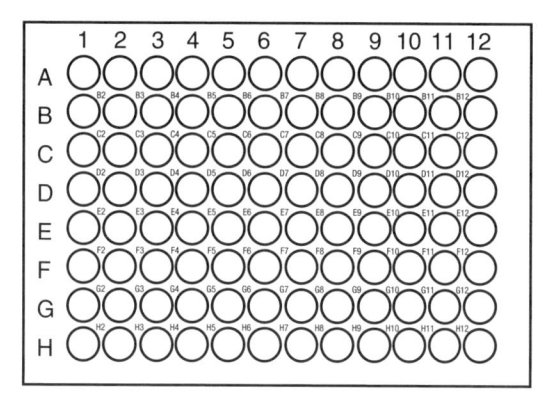

**Figure 2.** Lettering and Numbering in a 96-Well Plate.

Teacher Notes

*For best results, we recommend that the pipets and pipet labels be prepared ahead of time for the students. Because of the potential for contamination, teachers may also want to refill the pipets as needed before lab.*

Teacher Notes

## Precipitation Reactions

6. Place 4–5 drops of aluminum nitrate solution, the first "cation testing solution," $Al(NO_3)_3$, into well A1. Hold the pipet vertically to ensure uniform drops. Continue adding 4–5 drops of aluminum nitrate solution to the next five wells in column 1 (wells B1–F1).

7. Using the data table as a guide, place 4–5 drops of the appropriate "cation testing solution" into the first six wells in each vertical column 2–8 (ammonium nitrate into wells A2–F2, barium nitrate into wells A3–F3, etc.). *Note:* Consult the data table frequently and carefully read each label to avoid filling wells with the wrong solution.

8. Add 4–5 drops of sodium carbonate solution, the first "anion testing solution," $Na_2CO_3$, into well A1.

9. If a precipitate forms or the mixture appears cloudy, write PPT in the correct circle in the data table. If no precipitate forms, write NR (no reaction) in the circle. Remember that not all pairs of solutions will react, and that sometimes the precipitate may take a minute to develop. Use a *clean* toothpick to stir the mixture if the result is not obvious.

10. Continue adding sodium carbonate solution to each filled well in row A (wells A2–A8). When all of the mixtures have been made, go back and record any evidence of reaction in each well as PPT or NR, as described in step 9.

11. In the same manner, add the appropriate "anion testing solution" to each filled well in its row, as shown in the data table (sodium chloride to wells B1–B8, sodium hydroxide to wells C1–C8, etc.) *Note:* Consult the data table frequently and carefully read each label to avoid filling wells with the wrong solution.

12. Record any evidence of reaction in each well as PPT or NR. If there is any doubt about the observations in any well, repeat that test in an empty well on the reaction plate.

## Disposal

13. Some of the transition metal and other heavy metal salts used in this experiment should not be discarded into the water supply. Dump the contents of the 96-well reaction plate onto folded paper towels and discard the used paper towels in the wastebasket.

14. Use cotton swabs to clean out any remaining residues in the reaction plate. Thoroughly rinse the reaction plate several times with distilled water.

*If a precipitate appears to be very faint or if the solution appears cloudy, advise students to try to read a line of type through the well. If the type cannot be read, assume that a precipitate has formed.*

**Double Replacement Reactions and Solubility** – Page 6

Name: _____

Class/Lab Period: _____

# Double Replacement Reactions

**Data Table**

|  | Al(NO₃)₃ | NH₄NO₃ | Ba(NO₃)₂ | Ca(NO₃)₂ | Cu(NO₃)₂ | Fe(NO₃)₃ | AgNO₃ | Zn(NO₃)₂ |
|---|---|---|---|---|---|---|---|---|
| Na₂CO₃ | A1 | A2 | A3 | A4 | A5 | A6 | A7 | A8 |
| NaCl | B1 | B2 | B3 | B4 | B5 | B6 | B7 | B8 |
| NaOH | C1 | C2 | C3 | C4 | C5 | C6 | C7 | C8 |
| NaI | D1 | D2 | D3 | D4 | D5 | D6 | D7 | D8 |
| Na₃PO₄ | E1 | E2 | E3 | E4 | E5 | E6 | E7 | E8 |
| Na₂SO₄ | F1 | F2 | F3 | F4 | F5 | F6 | F7 | F8 |

Teacher Notes

Flinn ChemTopic™ Labs — Chemical Reactions

*Page 7 –* **Double Replacement Reactions and Solubility**

Teacher Notes

**Post-Lab Questions** *(Use a separate sheet of paper to answer the following questions.)*

1. For each combination of an anion and cation testing solution that produced a precipitate, write the name and formula of the solid product. *Hint:* Recall that all sodium salts and all nitrate salts are soluble. Remember to balance the positive and negative charges in the formulas of the products.

2. Write both a balanced molecular equation and a net ionic equation for each precipitation reaction observed in this experiment.

3. (a) Which anion testing solutions produced the fewest (<3) precipitates?

   (b) Salts of these anions may be described as soluble with only a few exceptions. Name the cations that are the *exceptions* to the rule for each anion identified in 3a.

4. (a) Which anion testing solutions produced the most (>5) precipitates?

   (b) Salts of these anions may be described as insoluble with only a few exceptions. Name the cations that are *exceptions* to the rule for each anion identified in 4a.

5. Although you did not test the bromide ($Br^-$) anion, would you expect most bromide salts ($AlBr_3$, $NH_4Br$, $BaBr_2$, etc.) to be soluble or insoluble? What is the likely exception to this rule? *Hint:* Use the periodic table to see which of the anions you tested would behave like bromide.

6. Complete the following table to summarize the general solubility rules of ionic compounds. Two entries have been filled in for you.

| Ionic Compounds | Soluble or Insoluble | Exceptions |
| --- | --- | --- |
| **Carbonates** | | |
| **Chlorides, Bromides, and Iodides** | | |
| **Hydroxides** | | |
| **Nitrates** | Soluble | None |
| **Phosphates** | | |
| **Sulfates** | | |
| **Alkali Metal Salts ($Na^+$, $K^+$, etc.)** | Soluble | None |
| **Ammonium Salts** | | |

**Teacher's Notes**

# Teacher's Notes
## Double Replacement Reactions and Solubility

*Microscale*

**Master Materials List** (for a class of 30 students working in pairs)

*Anion Testing Solutions, 0.1 M*
Sodium carbonate, $Na_2CO_3$, 45 mL
Sodium chloride, NaCl, 45 mL
Sodium hydroxide, NaOH, 45 mL
Sodium iodide, NaI, 45 mL
Sodium phosphate, $Na_3PO_4$, 45 mL
Sodium sulfate, $Na_2SO_4$, 45 mL

*Cation Testing Solutions, 0.1 M*
Aluminum nitrate, $Al(NO_3)_3$, 30 mL
Ammonium nitrate, $NH_4NO_3$, 30 mL
Barium nitrate, $Ba(NO_3)_2$, 30 mL
Calcium nitrate, $Ca(NO_3)_2$, 30 mL
Copper(II) nitrate, $Cu(NO_3)_2$, 30 mL
Iron(III) nitrate, $Fe(NO_3)_3$, 30 mL
Silver nitrate, $AgNO_3$, 30 mL
Zinc nitrate, $Zn(NO_3)_2$, 30 mL

*Equipment*
Cotton swabs
Distilled water
Labels, adhesive, 1" × 2⅝", 210
Paper, black, 15 sheets
Paper towels
Pipets, thin stem, 210

Pipet holders (24-well plates), 15
Reaction plates, 96-well, 15
Toothpicks, 1 box
Wash bottles, 15

**Preparation of Solutions** (for two classes of 30 students working in pairs)

**Table 1.** Amount of solid needed to prepare 100 mL of solution.

| Solution, 0.1 M | Reagent | Amount |
|---|---|---|
| Sodium Carbonate | $Na_2CO_3$ | 1.06 g |
| Sodium Chloride | NaCl | 0.58 g |
| Sodium Hydroxide | NaOH | 0.40 g |
| Sodium Iodide | NaI | 1.50 g |
| Sodium Phosphate | $Na_3PO_4 \cdot 12H_2O$ | 3.80 g |
| Sodium Sulfate | $Na_2SO_4$ | 1.42 g |
| Aluminum Nitrate | $Al(NO_3)_3 \cdot 9H_2O$ | 3.75 g |
| Ammonium Nitrate | $NH_4NO_3$ | 0.80 g |
| Barium Nitrate | $Ba(NO_3)_2$ | 2.61 g |
| Calcium Nitrate | $Ca(NO_3)_2 \cdot 4H_2O$ | 2.36 g |
| Copper(II) Nitrate | $Cu(NO_3)_2 \cdot 3H_2O$ | 2.42 g |
| Iron(III) Nitrate | $Fe(NO_3)_3 \cdot 9H_2O$ | 4.04 g |
| Silver Nitrate | $AgNO_3$ | 1.70 g |
| Zinc Nitrate | $Zn(NO_3)_2 \cdot 6H_2O$ | 2.98 g |

Teacher Notes

*Rinse the labeled pipets after use and store them in sealed plastic bags for reuse in future years.*

Flinn ChemTopic™ Labs — Chemical Reactions

# Teacher's Notes

Teacher Notes

## Safety Precautions

*Ammonium nitrate, barium nitrate, copper(II) nitrate, and silver nitrate solutions are slightly toxic by ingestion. Silver nitrate, sodium carbonate, and sodium hydroxide solutions are skin and eye irritants; silver nitrate will also stain skin and clothing. Avoid contact of all chemicals with eyes and skin. Wear chemical splash goggles and chemical-resistant gloves and apron. Please consult current Material Safety Data Sheets for additional safety, handling, and disposal information. Remind students to wash their hands thoroughly with soap and water before leaving the lab.*

## Disposal

Consult your current *Flinn Scientific Catalog/Reference Manual* for general guidelines and specific procedures governing the disposal of laboratory waste. The small amounts of insoluble transition metal and other toxic salts generated in this experiment may be safely discarded in the solid waste according to Flinn Suggested Disposal Method #26a. (See steps 13 and 14 on page 21.) Do not dispose of excess anion and cation testing solutions. Store these solutions in properly labeled and capped bottles for use the following year.

## Lab Hints

- The laboratory work for this experiment can be completed within a typical 50-minute lab period if solutions are readily available and easily dispensed. With so many solutions to combine, it is important for students to be well prepared in advance of lab. Keep distractions to a minimum in order to avoid contamination of the 14 different testing solutions. Allow students to work at their own pace and to repeat tests if they are unsure of the results or if they feel they have inadvertently mixed up solutions.

- To avoid contamination, we recommend that teachers fill and refill the pipets. If students will be filling the pipets, set up several dispensing stations around the lab to relieve congestion. Three or four dispensing stations per room are optimum for a class of 24 students working in pairs.

- The procedure as written calls for 96-well (8 × 12) reaction plates and about 10 drops total solution volume in each well. The microscale procedure allows all precipitation reactions to be easily observed and reduces the amount of solutions that must be prepared as well as any potential hazard and disposal problems. The microscale amounts may pose a challenge for some students. The procedure may be revised to use larger, 48-well (6 × 8) reaction plates and 20 drops total solution volume in each well.

- Many teachers do precipitation labs such as this one on a piece of write-on acetate (such as the transparency sheets sold for use with overhead projectors). Students use just 1–2 drops of each reagent and surface tension keeps the drops nice and round. Cleanup is very easy—simply wipe the acetate clean with a paper towel. See the *Supplementary Information* section for a full-size transparency master that can be used either as a reaction guide or as a data table.

# Teacher's Notes

- The number of anion and cation testing solutions has been kept to a deliberate minimum to avoid using toxic heavy metals (e.g., cobalt, nickel, mercury, and lead cation testing solutions, as well as sodium chromate) that would require dedicated heavy metal waste disposal. The number of testing solutions may be increased, if desired, to give students a wider range of examples for the solubility rules. Additional anion testing solutions that may be used include sodium bromide, sodium iodate, and sodium oxalate. Additional cation testing solutions that may be used include potassium nitrate, magnesium nitrate, strontium nitrate, and manganese(II) chloride.

## Teaching Tips

- Many procedures for analyzing the purity of compounds are based on precipitation reactions (gravimetric analysis). For example, the amount of chloride ion is determined by precipitation of silver chloride, while barium is determined by precipitation of barium sulfate. Dietary calcium and iron tablets are analyzed for their mineral content by precipitation of calcium oxalate and iron oxide, respectively. Discuss with students the experimental modifications that would be important in order to adapt precipitation reactions for analytical purposes (using excess precipitating agents, ensuring quantitative transfer and filtration techniques, avoiding interference due to other ions, etc.).

- Precipitation reactions also have applications in soil chemistry (knowing which compounds will precipitate when water containing dissolved minerals from agricultural runoff is passed through soils) and in physiological chemistry (understanding that fluoride salts are toxic because fluoride precipitates with calcium in bones and teeth).

## Answers to Pre-Lab Questions *(Student answers will vary.)*

1. Read the entire *Procedure,* including the *Safety Precautions*. Which solutions used in this experiment are described as skin and eye irritants? What does this mean? What precautions are used to protect against these hazards?

    *Silver nitrate, sodium carbonate, and sodium hydroxide solutions are skin and eye irritants. Skin and eye contact with all chemicals should be avoided by wearing chemical-resistant gloves and, of course, chemical splash goggles, whenever working with chemicals in the lab. It is also a good practice to routinely wash hands with soap and water after working in the lab.* **Note to teachers:** *Symptoms of localized skin and eye irritation include stinging, redness, and dryness. Some chemicals may also cause an allergic reaction, resulting in a skin rash. The eyes are especially sensitive to chemical irritants.*

2. Solutions of calcium, zinc, and lead nitrate were mixed pairwise with sodium iodide, sodium sulfate, and sodium chromate using the procedure described in this experiment (see the following table of results). Write a molecular equation and a net ionic equation for each double replacement reaction that produced a precipitate.

*Continued on page 27*

**Teacher's Notes**

Teacher Notes

|  | Calcium Nitrate, $Ca(NO_3)_2$ | Lead Nitrate, $Pb(NO_3)_2$ | Zinc Nitrate, $Zn(NO_3)_2$ |
|---|---|---|---|
| **Sodium Chromate, $Na_2CrO_4$** | PPT | PPT | PPT |
| **Sodium Iodide, NaI** | NR | PPT | NR |
| **Sodium Sulfide, $Na_2S$** | NR | PPT | PPT |

*Calcium:* $Ca(NO_3)_2(aq) + Na_2CrO_4(aq) \rightarrow CaCrO_4(s) + 2NaNO_3(aq)$
$Ca^{2+}(aq) + CrO_4^{2-}(aq) \rightarrow CaCrO_4(s)$

*Lead:* $Pb(NO_3)_2(aq) + Na_2CrO_4(aq) \rightarrow PbCrO_4(s) + 2NaNO_3(aq)$
$Pb^{2+}(aq) + CrO_4^{2-}(aq) \rightarrow PbCrO_4(s)$

$Pb(NO_3)_2(aq) + 2NaI(aq) \rightarrow PbI_2(s) + 2NaNO_3(aq)$
$Pb^{2+}(aq) + 2I^-(aq) \rightarrow PbI_2(s)$

$Pb(NO_3)_2(aq) + Na_2S(aq) \rightarrow PbS(s) + 2NaNO_3(aq)$
$Pb^{2+}(aq) + S^{2-}(aq) \rightarrow PbS(s)$

*Zinc:* $Zn(NO_3)_2(aq) + Na_2CrO_4(aq) \rightarrow ZnCrO_4(s) + 2NaNO_3(aq)$
$Zn^{2+}(aq) + CrO_4^{2-}(aq) \rightarrow ZnCrO_4(s)$

$Zn(NO_3)_2(aq) + Na_2S(aq) \rightarrow ZnS(s) + 2NaNO_3(aq)$
$Zn^{2+}(aq) + S^{2-}(aq) \rightarrow ZnS(s)$

3. What are the advantages and disadvantages of using molecular equations, complete ionic equations, and net ionic equations to describe double replacement reactions?

| Chemical Equation | Advantages | Disadvantages |
|---|---|---|
| **Molecular Equation** | Formulas of reactants and products tell you what compounds are combined. | Does not show that the reaction occurs between ions dissolved in solution. |
| **Complete Ionic Equation** | Illustrates that the reaction takes place between ions dissolved in solution. | With all ions listed, it may be hard to focus on which ones are most relevant. |
| **Net Ionic Equation** | Succinctly describes the combination of ions to produce the precipitate. | Does not indicate the actual compounds used in the reaction. |

Double Replacement Reactions and Solubility

# Teacher's Notes

## Sample Data

*Student data may vary.*

### Data Table

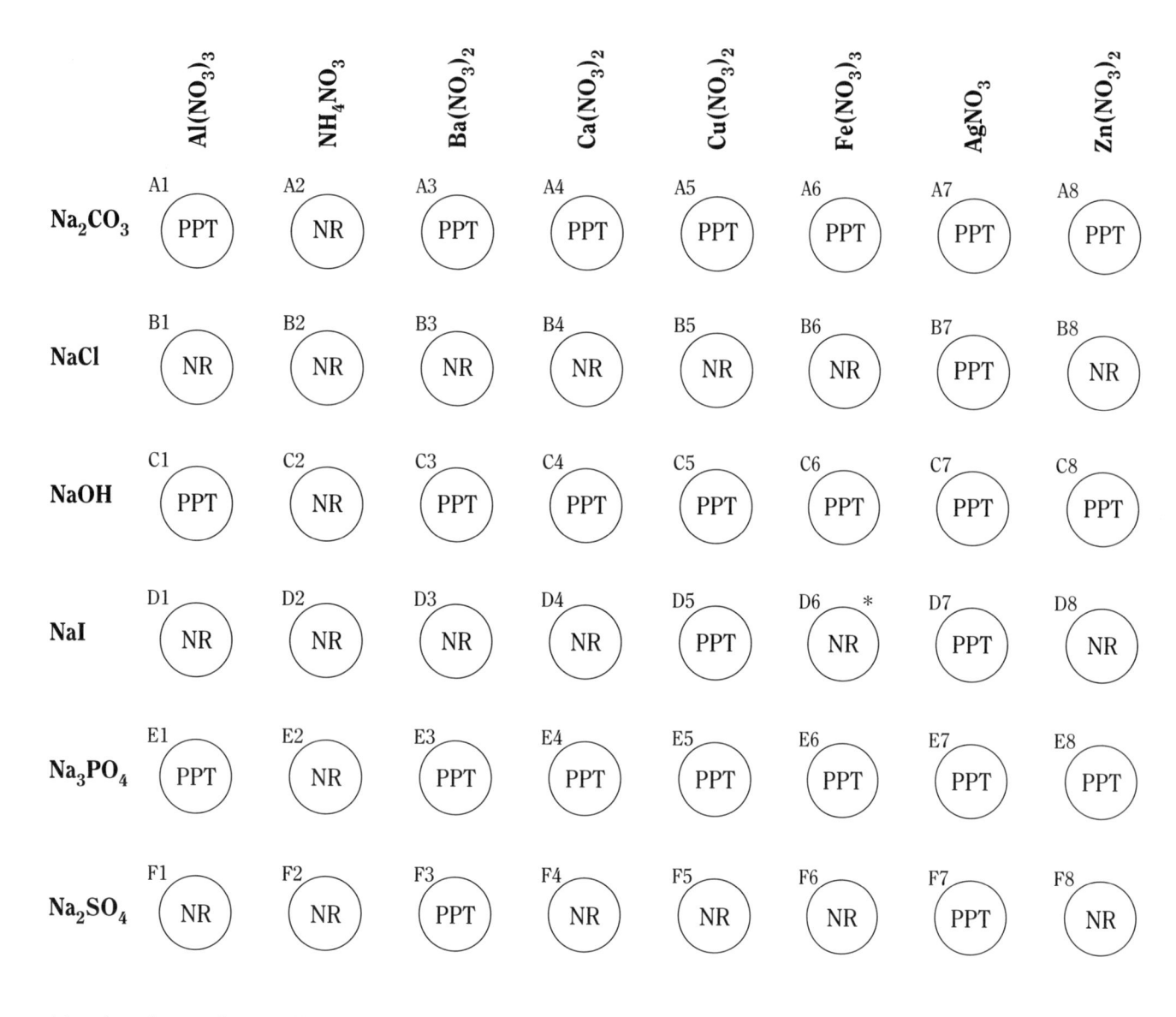

|  | Al(NO$_3$)$_3$ | NH$_4$NO$_3$ | Ba(NO$_3$)$_2$ | Ca(NO$_3$)$_2$ | Cu(NO$_3$)$_2$ | Fe(NO$_3$)$_3$ | AgNO$_3$ | Zn(NO$_3$)$_2$ |
|---|---|---|---|---|---|---|---|---|
| Na$_2$CO$_3$ | A1 PPT | A2 NR | A3 PPT | A4 PPT | A5 PPT | A6 PPT | A7 PPT | A8 PPT |
| NaCl | B1 NR | B2 NR | B3 NR | B4 NR | B5 NR | B6 NR | B7 PPT | B8 NR |
| NaOH | C1 PPT | C2 NR | C3 PPT | C4 PPT | C5 PPT | C6 PPT | C7 PPT | C8 PPT |
| NaI | D1 NR | D2 NR | D3 NR | D4 NR | D5 PPT | D6 NR * | D7 PPT | D8 NR |
| Na$_3$PO$_4$ | E1 PPT | E2 NR | E3 PPT | E4 PPT | E5 PPT | E6 PPT | E7 PPT | E8 PPT |
| Na$_2$SO$_4$ | F1 NR | F2 NR | F3 PPT | F4 NR | F5 NR | F6 NR | F7 PPT | F8 NR |

*A color change from yellow to dark red is observed in well D6 when NaI is added to Fe(NO$_3$)$_3$. The color change is due to oxidation of I$^-$ ions to I$_2$.

---

**Teacher Notes**

*Barium hydroxide (well C3) is usually characterized as either slightly or moderately soluble. Barium hydroxide solution rapidly absorbs carbon dioxide from the air to form insoluble barium carbonate. In well A6, the apparent precipitate of iron(III) carbonate is probably due to iron(III) hydroxide instead. Iron(III) hydroxide in well C6 is best described as "hydrous ferric oxide," Fe$_2$O$_3$·nH$_2$O.*

**Teacher's Notes**

Teacher Notes

**Answers to Post-Lab Questions** *(Student answers will vary.)*

1. For each combination of an anion and cation testing solution that produced a precipitate, write the name and formula of the solid product. *Hint:* Recall that all sodium salts and all nitrate salts are soluble. Remember to balance the positive and negative charges in the formulas of the solids.

    | | |
    |---|---|
    | Well A1: | Aluminum carbonate, $Al_2(CO_3)_3$ |
    | Well A3: | Barium carbonate, $BaCO_3$ |
    | Well A4: | Calcium carbonate, $CaCO_3$ |
    | Well A5: | Copper(II) carbonate, $CuCO_3$ |
    | Well A6: | Iron(III) carbonate, $Fe_2(CO_3)_3$ |
    | Well A7: | Silver carbonate, $Ag_2CO_3$ |
    | Well A8: | Zinc carbonate, $ZnCO_3$ |

    Well B7: Silver chloride, $AgCl$

    | | | |
    |---|---|---|
    | Well C1: | Aluminum hydroxide, $Al(OH)_3$ | |
    | Well C3: | Barium hydroxide, $Ba(OH)_2$ | ***Note to teachers***: Slightly soluble. |
    | Well C4: | Calcium hydroxide, $Ca(OH)_2$ | ***Note to teachers***: Slightly soluble. |
    | Well C5: | Copper(II) hydroxide, $Cu(OH)_2$ | |
    | Well C6: | Iron(III) hydroxide, $Fe(OH)_3$ | |
    | Well C7: | Silver hydroxide, $AgOH$ | |

    ***Note to teachers***: "Silver hydroxide" exists in equilibrium with silver oxide, $Ag_2O$, a black solid.

    Well C8: Zinc hydroxide, $Zn(OH)_2$

    Well D5: Copper(II) iodide, $CuI_2$

    ***Note to teachers***: Copper(II) iodide does not exist. A redox reaction between $Cu^{2+}$ and $I^-$ ions produces elemental copper, $Cu(s)$, and iodine, $I_2$. A similar redox reaction occurs in well D6 between $Fe^{3+}$ and $I^-$ ions, where the products are $Fe^{2+}$ ions and iodine. A color change but not a precipitate is observed in D6.

    Well D7: Silver iodide, $AgI$

    | | |
    |---|---|
    | Well E1: | Aluminum phosphate, $AlPO_4$ |
    | Well E3: | Barium phosphate, $Ba_3(PO_4)_2$ |
    | Well E4: | Calcium phosphate, $Ca_3(PO_4)_2$ |
    | Well E5: | Copper(II) phosphate, $Cu_3(PO_4)_2$ |
    | Well E6: | Iron(III) phosphate, $FePO_4$ |
    | Well E7: | Silver phosphate, $Ag_3PO_4$ |
    | Well E8: | Zinc phosphate, $Zn_3(PO_4)_2$ |

*In cases where the compounds are reported to be slightly soluble, students may or may not observe a precipitate, depending on reaction conditions. These compounds generally give cloudy mixtures or traces of a precipitate.*

**Teacher's Notes**

Well F3:     Barium sulfate, $BaSO_4$

Well F7:     Silver sulfate, $Ag_2SO_4$    **Note to teachers:** Slightly soluble.

2. Write a balanced molecular equation and a net ionic equation for each precipitation reaction observed in this experiment.

Well A1:     $2Al(NO_3)_3(aq) + 3Na_2CO_3(aq) \rightarrow Al_2(CO_3)_3(s) + 6NaNO_3(aq)$
           $2Al^{3+}(aq) + 3CO_3^{2-}(aq) \rightarrow Al_2(CO_3)_3(s)$

Well A3:     $Ba(NO_3)_2(aq) + Na_2CO_3(aq) \rightarrow BaCO_3(s) + 2NaNO_3(aq)$
           $Ba^{2+}(aq) + CO_3^{2-}(aq) \rightarrow BaCO_3(s)$

Well A4:     $Ca(NO_3)_2(aq) + Na_2CO_3(aq) \rightarrow CaCO_3(s) + 2NaNO_3(aq)$
           $Ca^{2+}(aq) + CO_3^{2-}(aq) \rightarrow CaCO_3(s)$

Well A5:     $Cu(NO_3)_2(aq) + Na_2CO_3(aq) \rightarrow CuCO_3(s) + 2NaNO_3(aq)$
           $Cu^{2+}(aq) + CO_3^{2-}(aq) \rightarrow CuCO_3(s)$

Well A6:     $2Fe(NO_3)_3(aq) + 3Na_2CO_3(aq) \rightarrow Fe_2(CO_3)_3(s) + 6NaNO_3(aq)$
           $2Fe^{3+}(aq) + 3CO_3^{2-}(aq) \rightarrow Fe_2(CO_3)_3(s)$

Well A7:     $2AgNO_3(aq) + Na_2CO_3(aq) \rightarrow Ag_2CO_3(s) + 2NaNO_3(aq)$
           $2Ag^+(aq) + CO_3^{2-}(aq) \rightarrow Ag_2CO_3(s)$

Well A8:     $Zn(NO_3)_2(aq) + Na_2CO_3(aq) \rightarrow ZnCO_3(s) + 2NaNO_3(aq)$
           $Zn^{2+}(aq) + CO_3^{2-}(aq) \rightarrow ZnCO_3(s)$

Well B7:     $AgNO_3(aq) + NaCl(aq) \rightarrow AgCl(s) + NaNO_3(aq)$
           $Ag^+(aq) + Cl^-(aq) \rightarrow AgCl(s)$

Well C1:     $Al(NO_3)_3(aq) + 3NaOH(aq) \rightarrow Al(OH)_3(s) + 3NaNO_3(aq)$
           $Al^{3+}(aq) + 3OH^-(aq) \rightarrow Al(OH)_3(s)$

Well C3:     $Ba(NO_3)_2(aq) + 2NaOH(aq) \rightarrow Ba(OH)_2(s) + 2NaNO_3(aq)$
           $Ba^{2+}(aq) + 2OH^-(aq) \rightarrow Ba(OH)_2(s)$   **Slightly soluble**

Well C4:     $Ca(NO_3)_2(aq) + 2NaOH(aq) \rightarrow Ca(OH)_2(s) + 2NaNO_3(aq)$
           $Ca^{2+}(aq) + 2OH^-(aq) \rightarrow Ca(OH)_2(s)$   **Slightly soluble**

Well C5:     $Cu(NO_3)_2(aq) + 2NaOH(aq) \rightarrow Cu(OH)_2(s) + 2NaNO_3(aq)$
           $Cu^{2+}(aq) + 2OH^-(aq) \rightarrow Cu(OH)_2(s)$

Well C6:     $Fe(NO_3)_3(aq) + 3NaOH(aq) \rightarrow Fe(OH)_3(s) + 3NaNO_3(aq)$
           $Fe^{3+}(aq) + 3OH^-(aq) \rightarrow Fe(OH)_3(s)$

Well C7:     $AgNO_3(aq) + NaOH(aq) \rightarrow AgOH(s) + NaNO_3(aq)$
           $Ag^+(aq) + OH^-(aq) \rightarrow AgOH(s)$

Well C8:     $Zn(NO_3)_2(aq) + 2NaOH(aq) \rightarrow Zn(OH)_2(s) + 2NaNO_3(aq)$
           $Zn^{2+}(aq) + 2OH^-(aq) \rightarrow Zn(OH)_2(s)$

Well D5:     $Cu(NO_3)_2(aq) + 2NaI(aq) \rightarrow CuI_2(s) + 2NaNO_3(aq)$
           $Cu^{2+}(aq) + 2I^-(aq) \rightarrow CuI_2(s)$

**Note to teachers:** Copper(II) iodide does not exist. A redox reaction between $Cu^{2+}$ and $I^-$ ions produces elemental copper, $Cu(s)$, and iodine, $I_2$.

# Teacher's Notes

Teacher Notes

Well D7: $AgNO_3(aq) + NaI(aq) \rightarrow AgI(s) + NaNO_3(aq)$
$Ag^+(aq) + I^-(aq) \rightarrow AgI(s)$

Well E1: $Al(NO_3)_3(aq) + Na_3PO_4(aq) \rightarrow AlPO_4(s) + 3NaNO_3(aq)$
$Al^{3+}(aq) + PO_4^{3-}(aq) \rightarrow AlPO_4(s)$

Well E3: $3Ba(NO_3)_2(aq) + 2Na_3PO_4(aq) \rightarrow Ba_3(PO_4)_2(s) + 6NaNO_3(aq)$
$3Ba^{2+}(aq) + 2PO_4^{3-}(aq) \rightarrow Ba_3(PO_4)_2(s)$

Well E4: $3Ca(NO_3)_2(aq) + 2Na_3PO_4(aq) \rightarrow Ca_3(PO_4)_2(s) + 6NaNO_3(aq)$
$3Ca^{2+}(aq) + 2PO_4^{3-}(aq) \rightarrow Ca_3(PO_4)_2(s)$

Well E5: $3Cu(NO_3)_2(aq) + 2Na_3PO_4(aq) \rightarrow Cu_3(PO_4)_2(s) + 6NaNO_3(aq)$
$3Cu^{2+}(aq) + 2PO_4^{3-}(aq) \rightarrow Cu_3(PO_4)_2(s)$

Well E6: $Fe(NO_3)_3(aq) + Na_3PO_4(aq) \rightarrow FePO_4(s) + 3NaNO_3(aq)$
$Fe^{3+}(aq) + PO_4^{3-}(aq) \rightarrow FePO_4(s)$

Well E7: $3AgNO_3(aq) + Na_3PO_4(aq) \rightarrow Ag_3PO_4(s) + 3NaNO_3(aq)$
$3Ag^+(aq) + PO_4^{3-}(aq) \rightarrow Ag_3PO_4(s)$

Well E8: $3Zn(NO_3)_2(aq) + 2Na_3PO_4(aq) \rightarrow Zn_3(PO_4)_2(s) + 6NaNO_3(aq)$
$3Zn^{2+}(aq) + 2PO_4^{3-}(aq) \rightarrow Zn_3(PO_4)_2(s)$

Well F3: $Ba(NO_3)_2(aq) + Na_2SO_4(aq) \rightarrow BaSO_4(s) + 2NaNO_3(aq)$
$Ba^{2+}(aq) + SO_4^{2-}(aq) \rightarrow BaSO_4(s)$

Well F7: $2AgNO_3(aq) + Na_2SO_4(aq) \rightarrow Ag_2SO_4(s) + 2NaNO_3(aq)$
$2Ag^+(aq) + SO_4^{2-}(aq) \rightarrow Ag_2SO_4(s)$ **Slightly soluble**

3. (a) Which anion testing solutions produced the fewest (<3) precipitates?

   (b) Salts of these anions may be described as soluble with only a few exceptions. Name the cations that are the *exceptions* to the rule for each anion identified in 3a.

   *(a) Chloride, iodides, and sulfates.*

   *(b) Chlorides are soluble; silver chloride is the exception.*
   *Iodides are soluble; silver iodide is the exception.*
   *Sulfates are soluble; barium sulfate and silver sulfate are the exceptions.*
   *(Silver sulfate is slightly soluble.)*

4. (a) Which anion testing solutions produced the most (>5) precipitates?

   (b) Salts of these anions may be described as insoluble with only a few exceptions. Name the cations that are *exceptions* to the rule for each anion identified in 4a.

   *(a) Carbonates, hydroxides, and phosphates.*

Double Replacement Reactions and Solubility

# Teacher's Notes

*(b) Carbonates are insoluble; ammonium carbonate is the exception.
Hydroxides are insoluble: ammonium hydroxide is the exception.
Barium hydroxide and calcium hydroxide are usually reported as moderately or slightly soluble.
Phosphates are insoluble: ammonium phosphate is the exception.*
**Note to teachers:** *Remind students that all sodium salts are soluble. The alkali metal salts are exceptions to the general insolubility of carbonates, hydroxides, and phosphates.*

5. Although you did not test the bromide (Br⁻) anion, would you expect most bromide salts (AlBr$_3$, NH$_4$Br, BaBr$_2$, etc.) to be soluble or insoluble? What is the likely exception to this rule? *Hint:* Use the periodic table to see which of the anions you tested would behave like bromide.

   *Most bromide salts are soluble in water. The exception is silver bromide.*

6. Complete the following table to summarize the general solubility rules of ionic compounds. Two entries have been filled in for you.

| Ionic Compounds | Soluble or Insoluble | Exceptions |
| --- | --- | --- |
| **Carbonates** | Insoluble | Alkali metals and NH$_4^+$ |
| **Chlorides, Bromides, and Iodides** | Soluble | Ag$^+$ |
| **Hydroxides** | Insoluble | Alkali metals and NH$_4^+$ |
| **Nitrates** | Soluble | None |
| **Phosphates** | Insoluble | Alkali metals and NH$_4^+$ |
| **Sulfates** | Soluble | Ba$^{2+}$ and Ag$^+$ |
| **Alkali Metal Salts (Na$^+$, K$^+$, etc.)** | Soluble | None |
| **Ammonium Salts** | Soluble | None |

**Note to teachers:** *Lead(II) and mercury(II) halides are insoluble; these ions are additional exceptions to the general solubility behavior of halide salts.*

# Teacher's Notes

Teacher Notes

## Supplementary Information

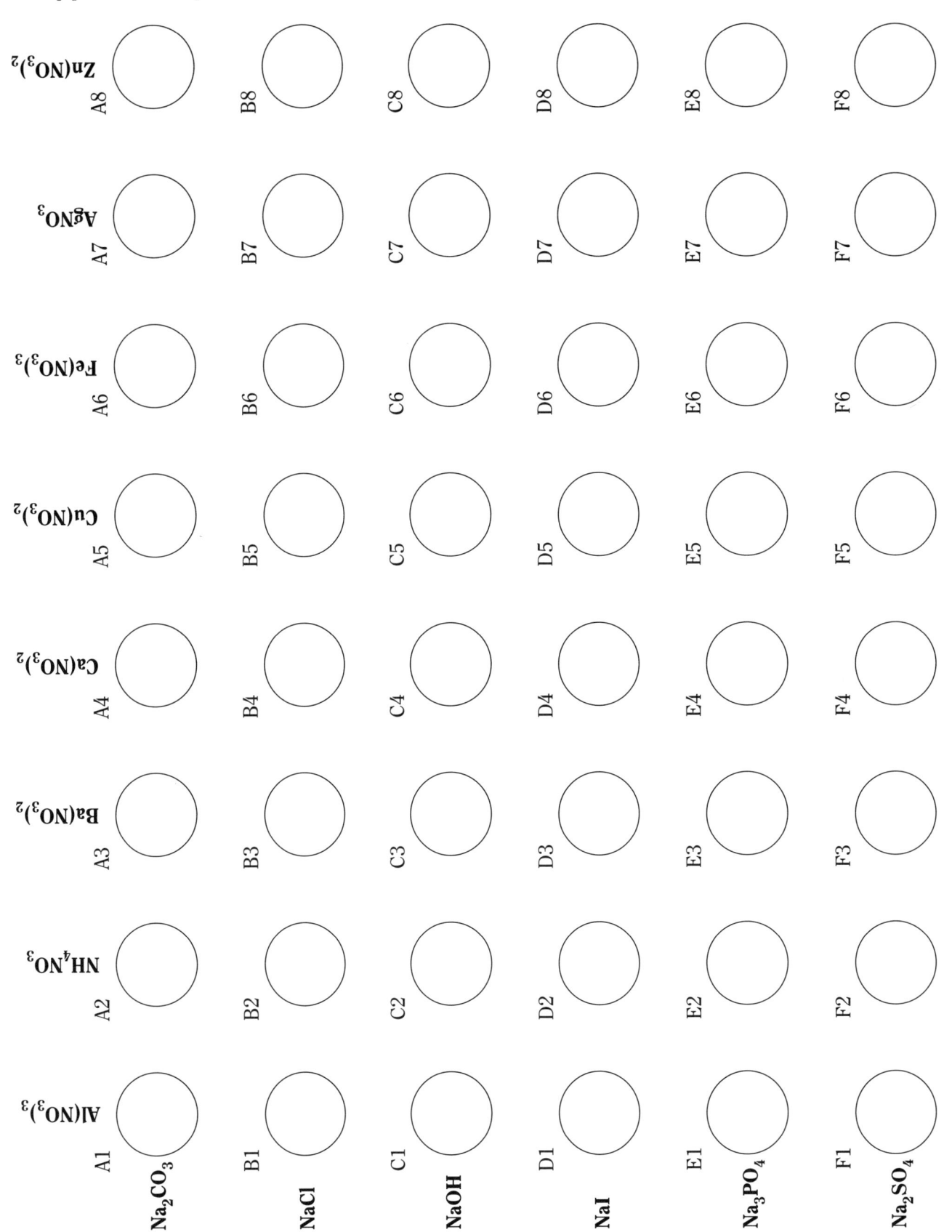

|   | A (Al(NO$_3$)$_3$) | B (NH$_4$NO$_3$) | C (Ba(NO$_3$)$_2$) | D (Ca(NO$_3$)$_2$) | E (Cu(NO$_3$)$_2$) | F (Fe(NO$_3$)$_3$) | G (AgNO$_3$) | H (Zn(NO$_3$)$_2$) |
|---|---|---|---|---|---|---|---|---|
| Na$_2$CO$_3$ | A1 | A2 | A3 | A4 | A5 | A6 | A7 | A8 |
| NaCl | B1 | B2 | B3 | B4 | B5 | B6 | B7 | B8 |
| NaOH | C1 | C2 | C3 | C4 | C5 | C6 | C7 | C8 |
| NaI | D1 | D2 | D3 | D4 | D5 | D6 | D7 | D8 |
| Na$_3$PO$_4$ | E1 | E2 | E3 | E4 | E5 | E6 | E7 | E8 |
| Na$_2$SO$_4$ | F1 | F2 | F3 | F4 | F5 | F6 | F7 | F8 |

*Copy this master table onto a sheet of acetate transparency for use as an alternative reaction sheet. (See the Lab Hints section.)*

Double Replacement Reactions and Solubility

# Teacher's Notes

**Teacher Notes**

# A Four-Reaction Copper Cycle
## Copper and Its Compounds

### Introduction

How old is the copper penny in your pocket? It may be older than you think! Not only is copper one of the most widely used metals, second only to iron in annual consumption, it is also the most widely reused metal. Almost as much copper is recovered every year from recycled copper scrap as is produced from newly mined copper ores. "Starting with copper, ending with copper" may well describe the applications of copper in industry. It also describes this experiment, in which a sequence of four chemical reactions will be used to demonstrate the properties of copper and its compounds.

### Concepts

- Oxidation–reduction
- Single replacement
- Double replacement
- Percent yield

### Background

Copper, a reddish-brown metal with excellent electrical and thermal conductivity, is the second most widely used metal in industry. Traditional applications of copper include its uses in wiring and plumbing. The modern electronics industry also depends on copper to make computers run faster and last longer. The utility of copper in these applications is enhanced because copper resists corrosion better than most metals. Copper also does not react readily with most strong acids.

Oxidation of copper takes place in concentrated nitric acid, a strong acid that is also a good oxidizing agent. Copper reacts with nitric acid to form copper(II) nitrate, a blue-green ionic compound that is soluble in water (Equation 1). Copper(II) nitrate, in turn, can be converted into other copper compounds via double replacement reactions with a variety of precipitating agents (Equation 2). Single replacement reactions of copper(II) compounds with more active metals, such as aluminum, magnesium or zinc, offer a means of regenerating copper metal (Equation 3).

*Oxidation of copper*

$$Cu(s) + 4HNO_3(aq) \rightarrow Cu(NO_3)_2(aq) + 2NO_2(g) + 2H_2O(l) \quad \text{Equation 1}$$

*Double replacement reaction*

$$Cu(NO_3)_2(aq) + 2NaOH(aq) \rightarrow Cu(OH)_2(s) + 2NaNO_3(aq) \quad \text{Equation 2}$$

*Single replacement reaction*

$$Cu(NO_3)_2(aq) + Zn(s) \rightarrow Cu(s) + Zn(NO_3)_2(aq) \quad \text{Equation 3}$$

---

*Until a few years ago, the wiring interconnects in computer chips were made from aluminum rather than copper. It is only in the last few years that copper wire has begun to dominate in chips for high-speed computer processing. Using copper in high-performance chips makes computers and other electronics devices faster, smaller, and cheaper.*

# A Four-Reaction Copper Cycle – Page 2

## Experiment Overview

The purpose of this experiment is to carry out a sequence of chemical reactions illustrating the properties of copper and its compounds. The "copper cycle"—which starts with copper and ends with copper—demonstrates different types of chemical reactions and provides a great test of the law of conservation of mass and of laboratory efficiency.

## Pre-Lab Questions

Read the entire *Procedure* and the recommended *Safety Precautions* before answering the following questions.

1. Concentrated strong acids, such as hydrochloric and sulfuric acid, are severely corrosive to skin and eyes and require great care when working with them in the lab. What additional hazard arises in this experiment when working with nitric acid? What safety precaution will protect against this hazard?

2. The four-reaction copper cycle featured in this experiment is summarized below. Fill in the blanks to show the reagents that will be used in each step.

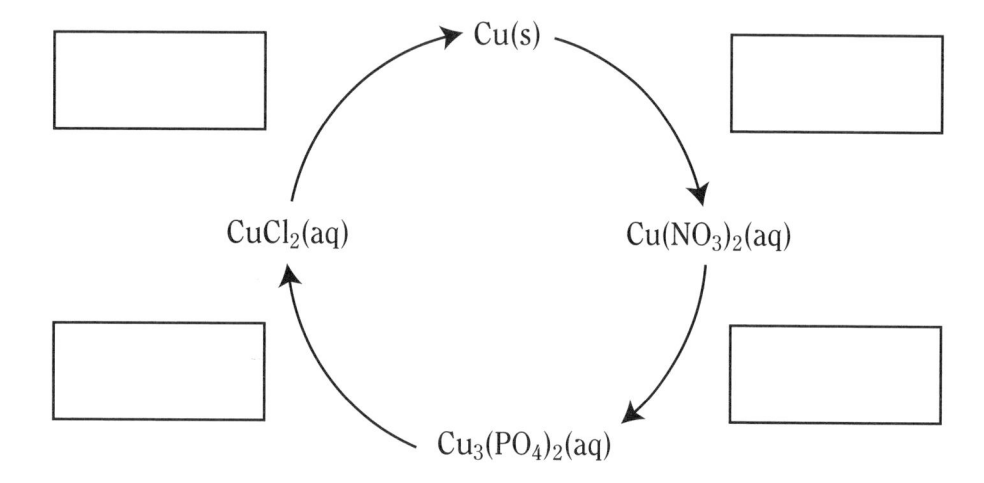

[Cycle diagram: Cu(s) → Cu(NO$_3$)$_2$(aq) → Cu$_3$(PO$_4$)$_2$(aq) → CuCl$_2$(aq) → Cu(s), with a blank box between each pair of species]

3. The amount of copper recovered at the end of the four-reaction cycle provides a good test of laboratory technique and efficiency. In order to obtain maximum recovery, each operation should be carried out without losing any copper. In Part B, copper(II) nitrate is converted to solid copper(II) phosphate, which is isolated by filtration. What observation might indicate that some of the copper was lost during this process?

*Page 3 –* **A Four-Reaction Copper Cycle**

Teacher Notes

## Materials

Acetone, 10 mL

Copper powder, Cu, 0.25–0.30 g

Hydrochloric acid, HCl, 3 M, 25 mL

Magnesium turnings, Mg, 0.6 g

Nitric acid, $HNO_3$, 6 M, 6 mL

Sodium hydroxide solution, NaOH, 6 M, 8 mL

Sodium phosphate solution, $Na_3PO_4$, 0.3 M, 10 mL

Water, distilled, and wash bottle

Balance, centigram (0.01-g precision)

Weighing dish

Beakers, 50- and 250-mL

Evaporating dish

Erlenmeyer flasks, 125-mL, 2

Funnel and filter paper

Graduated cylinders, 10- and 25-mL

Hot plate

pH paper

Pipets, Beral-type, 4

Spatula

Stirring rod

Tongs

## Safety Precautions

*Nitric acid is severely corrosive, a strong oxidizing agent, and toxic by ingestion and inhalation. Reactions of nitric acid with metals generate nitrogen dioxide, a toxic, reddish-brown gas. Work with nitric acid in a fume hood or a well-ventilated lab only. Hydrochloric acid is corrosive to skin and eyes and toxic by ingestion and inhalation. Sodium hydroxide solution is a corrosive liquid and can cause skin burns. It is especially dangerous to the eyes. Notify the teacher and clean up all acid and base spills immediately. Fine copper powder is a fire and explosion risk and a serious health hazard if inhaled as a dust or fume. Work carefully and avoid breathing copper powder. Acetone is a flammable solvent; avoid contact with flames and other sources of ignition. Work with acetone only in a well-ventilated lab. Avoid contact of all chemicals with eyes and skin. Wear chemical splash goggles and chemical-resistant gloves and apron. Wash hands thoroughly with soap and water before leaving the lab.*

## Procedure

### Part A. Copper and Nitric Acid

1. In a 50-mL beaker, weigh out 0.25–0.30 g of copper powder. Record the mass of copper to the nearest 0.01 g in the data table.

2. Place the beaker containing the copper in a fume hood. Using a Beral-type pipet, measure 6 mL of 6 M nitric acid in a graduated cylinder and carefully add the acid to the copper powder.

3. Observe the evidence for the chemical reaction and record all observations in the data table.

4. Gently swirl the beaker to make sure all of the copper has reacted. When the copper metal has dissolved, add 5 mL of distilled water to dilute the solution.

5. Take the beaker to the lab bench for Part B. *Caution:* Do not remove the beaker from the hood until all of the reddish-brown fumes have completely disappeared.

# A Four-Reaction Copper Cycle – *Page 4*

### Part B. Copper(II) Nitrate and Sodium Phosphate

6. Neutralize the acidic copper(II) nitrate solution: Slowly add 6–7 mL of 6 M sodium hydroxide with constant stirring until the mixture is *slightly* cloudy. *Note:* Copper(II) hydroxide will precipitate out instantaneously as a pale blue solid when the base is added. The precipitate will redissolve with stirring.

7. Test the solution with pH paper—the solution should be neutral or slightly acidic (pH 6–7). The solution should be almost clear, as well.

8. Measure 10 mL of 0.3 M sodium phosphate in a clean graduated cylinder and add it to the copper(II) nitrate solution in the beaker. Stir to mix thoroughly.

9. Observe the evidence for the chemical reaction and record all observations in the data table.

10. Prepare a funnel with filter paper for gravity filtration and place an Erlenmeyer flask beneath the funnel. Filter the reaction mixture.

11. Wash any traces of solid from the beaker into the funnel using a gentle stream of distilled water from a wash bottle.

12. Rinse the solid with about 5 mL of distilled water and discard the filtrate (liquid). Save the solid in the funnel for Part C. *Note:* The filtrate may be rinsed down the drain with excess water.

### Part C. Copper(II) Phosphate and Hydrochloric Acid

13. Place a clean 125-mL Erlenmeyer flask beneath the filter funnel.

14. Slowly and carefully pour 20 mL of 3 M HCl directly into the funnel and collect the filtrate in the Erlenmeyer flask. Record all observations in the data table.

15. When all of the solid on the filter paper has dissolved, rinse the filter with about 5 mL of distilled water and collect the rinse water in the same flask as the filtrate. Save the filtrate in the 125-mL Erlenmeyer flask for Part D.

### Part D. Copper(II) Chloride and Magnesium

16. Prepare a boiling water bath for use in step 26: Half-fill a 250-mL beaker with tap water, add a boiling stone, and heat the water to a gentle boil on a hot plate.

17. Obtain about 0.5 g of magnesium turnings in a weighing dish and add the magnesium to the filtrate from Part C. Observe the evidence for the chemical reaction and record all observations in the data table.

18. Swirl or stir the flask to complete the reaction. If the liquid does not turn colorless after 5–10 minutes, add another piece of magnesium turnings to the flask.

19. When the copper(II) chloride color has faded to colorless, add an extra 3 mL of 3 M hydrochloric acid to the flask. The acid will react with any leftover magnesium (but not with the copper).

---

**Teacher Notes**

*Review with students the proper procedure for setting up a funnel and filter paper and filtering a mixture. See the Laboratory Techniques Guide available from Flinn Scientific (Catalog No. AP6248) for a convenient student handout illustrating filtration and 15 other common laboratory techniques.*

## Teacher Notes

20. When the gas bubbling subsides, decant (pour off) most of the liquid into a waste beaker. Try not to lose any copper in the process.

21. Wash the copper with about 10 mL of distilled water and discard the wash water in the waste beaker.

22. Weigh a clean and dry evaporating dish and record the mass in the data table.

23. Use a gentle stream of water from a wash bottle to flush the copper from the Erlenmeyer flask into the evaporating dish.

24. Allow the copper to settle, then use a micro-tip pipet to remove most of the water from the evaporating dish.

25. Rinse the copper metal with two 5-mL portions of acetone. Remove the acetone rinses using a micro-tip pipet. *Caution:* There should be no open flames from laboratory burners in the lab where acetone is being used.

26. Place the evaporating dish over the boiling water bath and heat the copper to dryness.

27. Use tongs to remove the evaporating dish from the boiling water bath and place the dish on paper towels. Allow the dish to cool to room temperature and then thoroughly dry the dish using a paper towel.

28. Weigh the dry evaporating dish with the recycled copper and record the combined mass in the data table.

29. Dispose of the copper metal as directed by the instructor. Do not discard the copper down the drain.

---

*If microtip pipets are not available for steps 24 and 25, have students "pull" or draw out thin-stem pipets. Using a pipet to withdraw the liquid in steps 24 and 25 is more efficient than decanting the liquid, since some of the copper may be lost by decanting.*

Name: _____

Class/Lab Period: _____

# A Four-Reaction Copper Cycle

**Data Table**

| Part | Evidence of Chemical Reaction and Properties of Product(s) |
|---|---|
| A |  |
| B |  |
| C |  |
| D |  |

| | |
|---|---|
| Mass of Copper Metal (initial) | |
| Mass of Evaporating Dish | |
| Mass of Evaporating Dish + Copper | |

**Post-Lab Questions** *(Use a separate sheet of paper to answer the following questions.)*

1. Write a balanced chemical equation for each reaction in Parts A–D. Classify each reaction as a single replacement, double replacement, and/or oxidation–reduction reaction.

2. Calculate the mass of copper recovered at the end of the "four-reaction copper cycle" and the percent recovery of copper metal.

$$\text{Percent recovery} = \frac{\text{Mass of copper (final)}}{\text{Mass of copper (initial)}} \times 100\%$$

3. List at least three sources of experimental error that might lead to a mass of reclaimed copper less than that originally used. Be specific.

4. List at least three sources of experimental error that might lead to a mass of reclaimed copper greater than that originally used. Be specific.

---

Teacher Notes

*All single replacement reactions may also be classified as oxidation–reduction reactions. Not all oxidation–reduction reactions, however, are single replacement reactions.*

# Teacher's Notes
## A Four-Reaction Copper Cycle

**Master Materials List** *(for a class of 30 students working in pairs)*

Acetone, 150 mL
Copper powder, Cu, 4–5 g
Hydrochloric acid, HCl, 3 M, 400 mL
Magnesium turnings, Mg, 10 g
Nitric acid, $HNO_3$, 6 M, 100 mL
Sodium hydroxide solution, NaOH, 6 M, 100 mL
Sodium phosphate solution,
    $Na_3PO_4$, 0.3 M, 200 mL
Water, distilled, and wash bottles, 15
Balances, centigram, (0.01-g precision), 3
Beakers, 50- and 250-mL, 15

Evaporating dishes, 15
Erlenmeyer flasks, 125-mL, 30
Funnels and filter paper, 15
Graduated cylinders, 10- and 25-mL, 15
Hot plates, 5–7*
pH paper
Pipets, Beral-type, 60
Spatulas, 15
Stirring rods, 15
Tongs, 15
Weighing dishes, 15

*Several groups may share hot plates and boiling water baths.

**Preparation of Solutions** *(for a class of 30 students working in pairs)*

*Nitric Acid, 6 M:* Place about 50 mL of distilled or deionized water in a flask and slowly add 38 mL of concentrated (15.8 M) nitric acid. Stir to mix and then dilute to 100 mL with water. Note: Always add acid to water.

*Hydrochloric Acid, 3 M:* Place about 200 mL of distilled or deionized water in a flask and slowly add 125 mL of concentrated (12.1 M) hydrochloric acid. Stir to mix and then dilute to 500 mL with water. *Note:* Always add acid to water.

*Sodium Hydroxide, 6 M:* Cool a flask containing about 50 mL of distilled or deionized water in an ice-water bath and add 24 g of fresh sodium hydroxide pellets. Stir to dissolve and then dilute to 100 mL with water.

*Sodium Phosphate, 0.3 M:* Dissolve 28.5 g of sodium phosphate dodecahydrate ($Na_3PO_4 \cdot 12H_2O$) in 250 mL of distilled or deionized water.

**Safety Precautions**

*Nitric acid is severely corrosive, a strong oxidizing agent, and toxic by ingestion and inhalation. Reactions of nitric acid with metals evolve nitrogen dioxide, a toxic, reddish-brown gas. Work with nitric acid in a fume hood or a well-ventilated lab only. Hydrochloric acid is corrosive to skin and eyes and toxic by ingestion and inhalation. Sodium hydroxide solution is a corrosive liquid and can cause skin burns. It is especially dangerous to the eyes. Keep sodium carbonate and citric acid on hand to clean up acid and base spills, respectively. Fine copper powder is a fire and explosion risk and a serious health hazard if inhaled as a dust or fume. Work carefully and avoid breathing copper powder. Acetone is a flammable solvent; avoid contact with flames and other sources of ignition. Work with acetone only in a well-ventilated lab. Avoid contact of all chemicals with eyes and skin. Wear chemical splash*

# Teacher's Notes

*goggles and chemical-resistant gloves and apron. Please consult current Material Safety Data Sheets for additional safety, handling, and disposal information. Remind students to wash their hands thoroughly with soap and water before leaving the lab.*

## Disposal

Consult your current *Flinn Scientific Catalog/Reference Manual* for general guidelines and specific procedures governing the disposal of laboratory waste. The recycled copper obtained at the end of the experiment may be discarded in the trash according to Flinn Suggested Disposal Method #26a. Excess sodium hydroxide solution may be neutralized with acid and disposed of according to Flinn Suggested Disposal Method #10. Excess hydrochloric acid and nitric acid may be neutralized with base and disposed of according to Flinn Suggested Disposal Method #24b. The waste solution obtained at the end of Part D is acidic and should be neutralized with base and disposed of according to Flinn Suggested Disposal Method #24b. Set up an acetone waste beaker in the hood to collect the acetone rinses. Acetone may be allowed to evaporate in the hood according to Flinn Suggested Disposal Method #18a. Alternatively, the acetone rinse solvent may be saved and stored for future use.

## Lab Hints

- Many "copper cycle" experiments have been reported in the literature. The specific reactions in this lab were selected to improve the safety of the experiment and make it feasible to complete the cycle in one 50-minute lab period.

- This lab differs from common versions of the copper cycle experiment in two important ways. First, copper powder is substituted for copper wire, making it possible to use 6 M rather than concentrated nitric acid in Part A. Secondly, the resulting copper(II) nitrate is converted to copper(II) phosphate rather than to copper(II) hydroxide and then copper(II) oxide. Filtering or decanting a boiling hot mixture of copper(II) oxide is a potentially dangerous operation. This problem is eliminated when copper(II) phosphate is used as an intermediate in the copper cycle.

- Concentrated nitric acid is a serious health and safety hazard. Using copper powder makes it possible to use 6 M nitric acid as the dissolving reagent. The nitrogen dioxide fumes are substantially reduced with this substitution and the reaction time is still reasonable (about 10 minutes). Copper powder presents a minor dust and inhalation hazard, however, so teachers will want to consider this in choosing whether to carry out the reaction with copper powder or copper wire. Fine copper turnings may also react with 6 M $HNO_3$, although the reaction may take a little longer.

- If hood space is limited or laboratory ventilation is inadequate, teachers may want to demonstrate Part A to the students and prepare a stock solution of copper(II) nitrate for students to use directly in Part B. Starting with 20 mL of 0.20 M $Cu(NO_3)_2$ solution gives the same number of moles of copper as starting with 0.25 g of copper powder in Part A. Alternatively, teachers may give students one gram of solid copper(II) nitrate trihydrate (molar mass 241.6 g/mole) and instruct them to see how much copper metal they can recover from this solid.

*Flinn ChemTopic™ Labs* — Chemical Reactions

# Teacher's Notes

Teacher Notes

## Teaching Tips

- See the *Supplementary Information* section for a penny version of "Nitric Acid Acts on Copper—The First Demonstration." This demonstration is a tribute to Ira Remsen's well-known story of the reaction that motivated him to study chemistry.

- An advanced copper cycle experiment is available as a student laboratory kit from Flinn Scientific. "Sequence of Chemical Reactions" (Catalog No. AP5605) features a seven-reaction copper cycle—four 50-minute laboratory periods are recommended for its completion.

## Answers to Pre-Lab Questions *(Student answers will vary.)*

Read the entire *Procedure* and the recommended *Safety Precautions* before answering the following questions.

1. Concentrated strong acids, such as hydrochloric and sulfuric acid, are severely corrosive to skin and eyes and require great care when working with them in the lab. What additional hazard arises in this experiment when working with nitric acid? What safety precaution will protect against this hazard?

   *Reaction of copper metal with nitric acid generates nitrogen dioxide ($NO_2$), a toxic brown gas with an irritating odor. Part A should be carried out in the hood to avoid breathing $NO_2$ vapor.*

2. The four-reaction copper cycle featured in this experiment is summarized below. Fill in the blanks to show the reagents that will be used in each step.

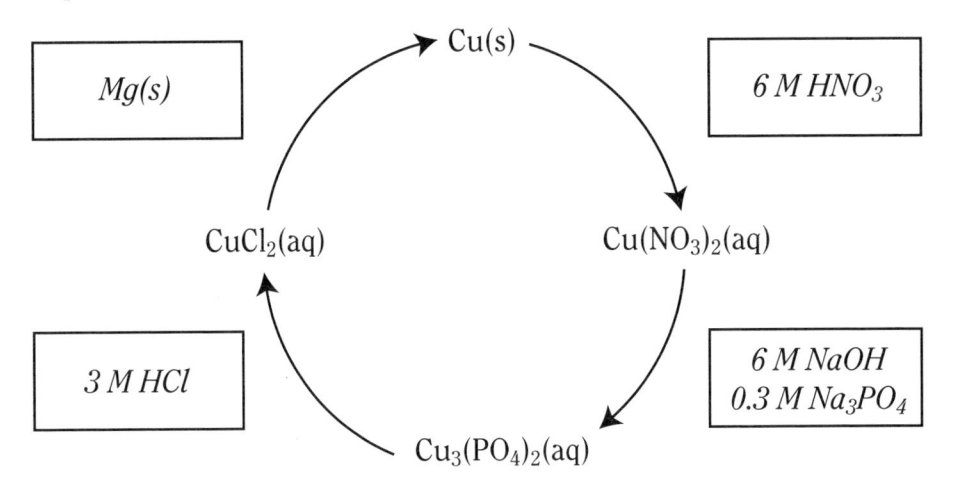

   Cycle diagram:
   - Cu(s) → [6 M $HNO_3$] → Cu($NO_3$)$_2$(aq)
   - Cu($NO_3$)$_2$(aq) → [6 M NaOH, 0.3 M $Na_3PO_4$] → $Cu_3(PO_4)_2$(aq)
   - $Cu_3(PO_4)_2$(aq) → [3 M HCl] → $CuCl_2$(aq)
   - $CuCl_2$(aq) → [Mg(s)] → Cu(s)

3. The amount of copper recovered at the end of the four-reaction cycle provides a good test of laboratory technique and efficiency. In order to obtain maximum recovery, each operation should be carried out without losing any copper. In Part B, copper(II) nitrate is converted to solid copper(II) phosphate, which is isolated by filtration. What observation might indicate that some of the copper was lost during this process?

   *The filtrate will be blue if any residual copper(II) compounds remain in solution. In order to avoid losing copper in Part B, the filtrate should be checked to make sure it is colorless.*

A Four-Reaction Copper Cycle

# Teacher's Notes

## Sample Data

*Student data will vary.*

### Data Table

| Part | Evidence of Chemical Reaction and Properties of Product(s) |
|---|---|
| A | Nitric acid bubbled as it was added to the copper metal and the liquid turned green, then blue. The solid copper dissolved and reddish brown fumes, which were quickly swept away in the fume hood exhaust, were observed. The beaker felt warm to the touch. It took about 5–10 minutes for the copper powder to completely dissolve. The final solution was blue. |
| B | Adding sodium hydroxide to the aqueous copper(II) nitrate solution gave an instantaneous, royal blue precipitate. This precipitate dissolved when the solution was stirred and the solution pH was about 6. Adding sodium phosphate gave a blue-green solid. The solid did not settle well and the final mixture had a milky appearance. Filtering the mixture gave a turquoise solid and a colorless filtrate. |
| C | The blue-green solid on the filter paper quickly dissolved when hydrochloric acid was added. The collected filtrate containing copper(II) chloride was greenish blue. No solid was left on the filter paper. |
| D | The solution bubbled vigorously when the magnesium was added and the flask got quite hot. A spongy red solid formed and quickly settled to the bottom of the flask. The blue color of the solution faded as the magnesium reacted. The solution turned colorless within 5 minutes (without adding any extra magnesium). Excess hydrochloric acid (3 mL) was added to dissolve any leftover magnesium—the solution fizzed slightly but the bubbling soon subsided. |
| **Mass of Copper Metal (initial)** | 0.29 g |
| **Mass of Evaporating Dish** | 41.23 g |
| **Mass of Evaporating Dish + Copper** | 41.44 g |

## Teacher's Notes

**Answers to Post-Lab Questions** *(Student answers will vary.)*

1. Write a balanced chemical equation for each reaction in Parts A–D. Classify each reaction as a single replacement, double replacement, and/or oxidation–reduction reaction.

   *Part A—Oxidation–reduction reaction*
   $Cu(s) + 4HNO_3(aq) \rightarrow Cu(NO_3)_2(aq) + 2NO_2(g) + 2H_2O(l)$

   *Part B—Double replacement (precipitation) reaction*
   $3Cu(NO_3)_2(aq) + 2Na_3PO_4(aq) \rightarrow Cu_3(PO_4)_2(s) + 6NaNO_3(aq)$

   *Part C—Double replacement (acid–base) reaction*
   $Cu_3(PO_4)_2(aq) + 6HCl(aq) \rightarrow 3CuCl_2(aq) + 2H_3PO_4(aq)$

   *Part D—Single replacement (oxidation–reduction) reaction*
   $CuCl_2(aq) + Mg(s) \rightarrow Cu(s) + MgCl_2(aq)$

2. Calculate the mass of copper recovered at the end of the "four-reaction copper cycle" and the percent recovery of copper metal.

   $$\text{Percent recovery} = \frac{\text{Mass of copper (final)}}{\text{Mass of copper (initial)}} \times 100\%$$

   *Mass of copper (final) = 41.44 g − 41.23 g = 0.21 g*

   *Percent recovery = (0.21 g/0.29 g) × 100% = 72%*

3. List at least three sources of experimental error that might lead to a mass of reclaimed copper less than that originally used. Be specific.

   *The following errors will lead to a mass of copper less than that originally used.*

   (a) *Not all of the copper powder reacted with nitric acid in Part A.*

   (b) *Some soluble copper(II) compound(s) remained dissolved in the filtrate in Part B.*

   (c) *Not all of the filtered copper(II) phosphate solid dissolved in hydrochloric acid in Part C.*

   (d) *Not enough magnesium was added or not enough time was allowed for all of the copper(II) chloride to react in Part D.*

   (e) *Any material was physically lost in the transfer steps in Parts A–D.*

# Teacher's Notes

4. List at least three sources of experimental error that might lead to a mass of reclaimed copper greater than that originally used. Be specific.

   *The following errors will lead to a mass of copper greater than that originally used.*

   (a) *The final copper sample is wet.*

   (b) *The final copper sample has been oxidized in moist air to CuO (due to a trace of acid remaining behind after washing).*

   (c) *The final copper sample is contaminated with magnesium because the excess magnesium was not dissolved at the end of Part D.*

## Supplementary Information

### Nitric Acid Acts Upon Copper—The First Demo

The story of Ira Remsen and his discovery of the reaction of nitric acid with copper has become a classic. Teachers love to retell the story as they recreate the demonstration that inspired the young Remsen "to learn more about that remarkable kind of action."

## Materials

Copper penny (pre-1983)  
Nitric acid, concentrated, $HNO_3$, 15 mL  
Water  
Erlenmeyer flask, 500 mL  
Graduated cylinder, 10-mL  
Paper towels

## Safety Precautions

*Nitric acid is a strong oxidizing agent and is severely corrosive to eyes, skin, and body tissue. Avoid contact with eyes and skin. Reaction of nitric acid with metals generates nitrogen dioxide, a toxic, reddish-brown gas with an irritating odor. Perform this demonstration in a hood or well-ventilated lab only. Wear chemical splash goggles and chemical-resistant gloves and apron.*

## Procedure

1. Work in the hood or a well-ventilated lab.

2. Moisten two or three paper towels with water and wring out the excess water. Fold the paper towels into a square.

3. Place a penny in the bottom of large Erlenmeyer flask and carefully add about 15 mL of concentrated nitric acid.

4. Quickly cover the Erlenmeyer flask with the damp, folded paper towels.

# Teacher's Notes

Teacher Notes

5. Observe the resulting chemical reaction while reading Ira Remsen's famous story of his first and most impressive experiment.

*"While reading a textbook on chemistry, I came upon the statement 'nitric acid acts upon copper.' I was getting tired of reading such absurd stuff and I determined to see what this meant. Copper was more or less familiar to me, for copper cents were then in use. I had seen a bottle marked 'nitric acid' on a table in the doctor's office where I was then 'doing time!' I did not know its peculiarities but I was getting on and likely to learn. The spirit of adventure was upon me. Having nitric acid and copper, I had only to learn what the words 'act upon' meant. Then the statement 'nitric acid acts upon copper' would be something more than mere words.*

*"All was still. In the interest of knowledge I was even willing to sacrifice one of the few copper cents then in my possession. I put one of them on the table; opened the bottle marked 'nitric acid'; poured some of the liquid on the copper; and prepared to make an observation.*

*"But what was this wonderful thing which I beheld? The cent was already changed, and it was no small change either. A greenish blue liquid foamed and fumed over the cent and over the table. The air in the neighborhood of the performance became dark red. A great colored cloud arose. This was disagreeable and suffocating—how should I stop this? I tried to get rid of the objectionable mess by picking it up and throwing it out of the window, which I had meanwhile opened. I learned another fact—nitric acid not only acts upon copper but it acts upon fingers. The pain led to another unpremeditated experiment. I drew my fingers across my trousers and another fact was discovered. Nitric acid also acts upon trousers.*

*"Taking everything into consideration, that was the most impressive experiment, and relatively, probably the most costly experiment I have ever performed. I tell of it even now with interest. It was a revelation to me. It resulted in a desire on my part to learn more about that remarkable kind of action. Plainly the only way to learn about it was to see its results, to experiment, to work in the laboratory."*

## Disposal

Please consult your current *Flinn Scientific Catalog/Reference Manual* for general guidelines and specific procedures governing the disposal of laboratory waste. The acidic waste solution contains copper nitrate. It may be neutralized with base and disposed of down the drain with excess water according to Flinn Suggested Disposal Method #10.

A Four-Reaction Copper Cycle

# Teacher's Notes

## Discussion

Ira Remsen (1846–1927) was an influential American chemist in the 19th and early 20th centuries. Trained as a physician in New York City, Remsen abandoned the practice of medicine soon after receiving his degree, choosing to pursue a passion for chemistry instead. After receiving a doctorate in organic chemistry in Germany in 1870, Ira Remsen returned to the United States, where he founded the chemistry department at Johns Hopkins University. He later served as president of the university as well. Credited with the co-discovery of the artificial sweetener saccharin, Ira Remsen left behind a rich legacy of research in organic chemistry. Remsen felt that his most important contribution, however, was not to research but to education, "to promote the study of pure science, to develop a scientific habit of mind in students and to train them to become investigators."

Given his devotion to chemistry education, Ira Remsen would be pleased to know that one story in particular from his lifetime of interest in chemistry has been passed down from generation to generation. Ira Remsen's memoir of his discovery of the properties of nitric acid has become an enduring symbol of the wonders of discovery in chemistry.

**Teacher Notes**

# Chemical Reactions and Qualitative Analysis
## An Inquiry Activity

## Introduction

To protect human health and safeguard the environment, the EPA regulates the amounts of many cations, including barium, copper, iron, lead, silver, and zinc, in drinking water. Precise *quantitative analysis* of these cations is achieved using special instruments. Sometimes, however, scientists merely want to know if these cations are present in water. This question can usually be answered by *qualitative analysis,* in which the possible impurities in water are separated from one another and then identified using a series of characteristic chemical reactions.

## Concepts

- Chemical reactions
- Precipitation reactions
- Qualitative analysis
- Complex ion reactions

## Background

Inorganic qualitative analysis of water involves carrying out a series of chemical reactions to test for the presence or absence of specific ions. In this experiment, you will design a qualitative analysis scheme for the separation and identification of three metal cations—iron(III) ($Fe^{3+}$), silver ($Ag^+$), and zinc ($Zn^{2+}$) ions. The cations can be separated from the mixture using *precipitation reactions* to selectively precipitate one cation. After the cations have been separated, they can be positively identified using characteristic *complex ion reactions* or additional precipitation reactions. Consider the following relevant chemical reactions of iron(III), silver, and zinc ions.

### Precipitation Reactions

$Fe^{3+}(aq) + HCl(aq) \rightarrow$ No Reaction

$Ag^+(aq) + HCl(aq) \rightarrow AgCl(s) + H^+(aq)$
  White

$Zn^{2+}(aq) + HCl(aq) \rightarrow$ No Reaction

$Fe^{3+}(aq) + 3NaOH(aq) \rightarrow Fe(OH)_3(s) + 3Na^+(aq)$
  Red

$2Ag^+(aq) + 2NaOH(aq) \rightarrow Ag_2O(s) + H_2O(l) + 2Na^+(aq)$
  Black

$Zn^{2+}(aq) + 2NaOH(aq) \rightarrow Zn(OH)_2(s) + 2Na^+(aq)$
  White

$3Zn^{2+}(aq) + 2K_4Fe(CN)_6(aq) \rightarrow Zn_3K_2[Fe(CN)_6]_2(s) + 6K^+(aq)$
  Gray-blue

### Complex Ion Reactions

$Zn^{2+}(aq) + 4NaOH(aq) \rightarrow Zn(OH)_4^{2-}(aq) + 4Na^+(aq)$

---

*Precipitation reactions are a subset of double replacement reactions (see the previous experiment "Double Replacement Reactions and Solubility" in this lab manual). Complex ion reactions represent a type of combination reaction of metal ions with ligands (either anionic or neutral) in solution.*

# Chemical Reactions and Qualitative Analysis – Page 2

$$AgCl(s) + 2NH_3(aq) \rightarrow Ag(NH_3)_2^+(aq) + Cl^-(aq)$$

$$Fe(OH)_3(s) + 3HCl(aq) + SCN^-(aq) \rightarrow \underset{Red}{FeSCN^{2+}(aq)} + 3Cl^-(aq) + 3H_2O(l)$$

$$Zn(OH)_4^{2-}(aq) + 4HCl(aq) \rightarrow Zn^{2+}(aq) + 4H_2O(l) + 4Cl^-(aq)$$

## Experiment Overview

The purpose of this experiment is to design and carry out a sequence of chemical reactions for the separation and identification of iron(III) ($Fe^{3+}$), silver ($Ag^+$), and zinc ($Zn^{2+}$) ions in water. Two parallel series of tests will be carried out, one with a known sample containing all three metal cations, the other with an unknown sample containing only one or two metals.

## Pre-Lab Questions

1. What precipitation reaction could be used to separate and remove silver ions from a mixture containing iron(III), silver, and zinc ions?

2. What precipitation reaction could be used to separate and remove iron(III) ions from the remaining mixture containing iron(III) and zinc ions?

3. How can the presence of silver ions be positively identified?

4. How can the presence of iron(III) ions be positively identified?

5. How can the presence of zinc ions be positively identified?

6. Complete the following flow chart.

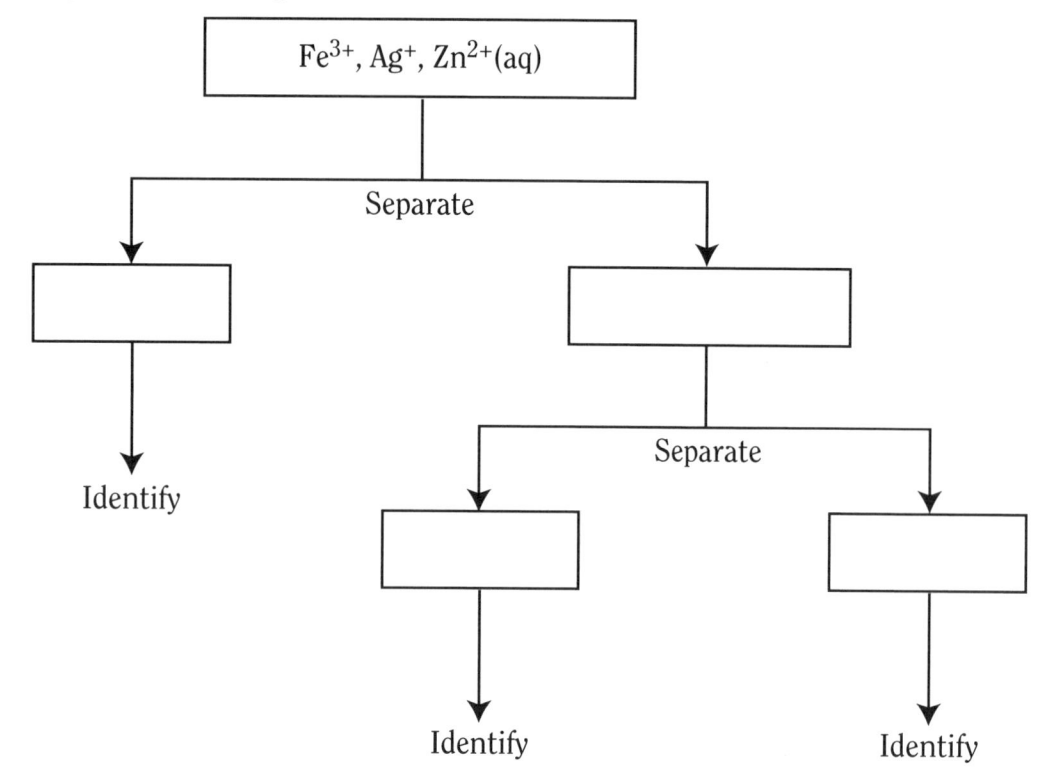

**Figure 1.** Qualitative Analysis of $Fe^{3+}$, $Ag^+$, and $Zn^{2+}$ Ions.

*Page 3* – **Chemical Reactions and Qualitative Analysis**

Teacher Notes

## Materials

"Known" sample for qualitative analysis, 3 mL
    Mixture of $Fe(NO_3)_3$, $AgNO_3$, and $Zn(NO_3)_2$ (0.05 M in each cation)

Reference samples for qualitative analysis (optional)
    Iron(III) nitrate, $Fe(NO_3)_3$, 0.05 M, 3 mL
    Silver nitrate, $AgNO_3$, 0.05 M, 3 mL
    Zinc nitrate, $Zn(NO_3)_2$, 0.05 M, 3 mL

"Unknown" sample for qualitative analysis, 3 mL

Ammonia (ammonium hydroxide) solution, $NH_3$, 6 M, 3 mL

Hydrochloric acid, HCl, 3 M, 3 mL

Potassium ferrocyanide solution, $K_4Fe(CN)_6$, 0.2 M, 1 mL

Potassium thiocyanate solution, KSCN, 0.2 M, 1 mL

Sodium hydroxide solution, NaOH, 6 M, 3 mL

Centrifuge

Litmus paper

Pipets, Beral-type, 10

Reaction plate, 24-well (optional)

Stirring rod

Stoppers, size 00 (to fit test tubes), 2

Test tubes, small, 6

Test tube rack

Water, distilled, and wash bottle

Wax pencil or permanent marker

## Safety Precautions

*Sodium hydroxide and ammonia solutions are corrosive liquids and especially dangerous to the eyes; skin burns are possible. Ammonia is also toxic by inhalation. Hydrochloric acid is toxic by ingestion and inhalation and is corrosive to skin and eyes. Silver nitrate solution is a skin and eye irritant and is slightly toxic by ingestion; iron(III) nitrate solution may also be irritating to body tissues. Potassium ferrocyanide and potassium thiocyanate solutions are slightly toxic by ingestion and may liberate toxic hydrogen cyanide gas upon contact with concentrated acids. Avoid contact of all chemicals with eyes and skin. Notify the teacher and clean up all spills immediately. Wear chemical splash goggles and chemical-resistant gloves and apron. Wash hands thoroughly with soap and water before leaving the lab.*

## General Techniques for Qualitative Analysis

- As the flow chart suggests, the number of solutions and precipitates increases as one proceeds through a qualitative analysis scheme. Keeping good records is essential for success. Number test tubes with a wax pencil or tape and permanent marker so the numbers will not rub off. Maintain a current, working record of observations and results—don't trust the results to memory.

# Chemical Reactions and Qualitative Analysis – Page 4

- It is not necessary to measure exact liquid volumes. Estimates are fine. Adding a few drops of a concentrated precipitating agent (e.g., 3 M HCl or 6 M NaOH) will give better results than using a larger volume of a more dilute solution.

- Tap water may be a source of contaminating ions. Rinse all glassware and pipets with distilled water before use. If using a stirring rod to mix solutions, rinse the stirring rod in distilled water before transferring it to a new solution.

- Separating a solid precipitate from the remaining liquid (called the supernatant) is a key step in qualitative analysis. This is best done by centrifuging the mixture for about 30 seconds—the solid will pack down into the bottom of the test tube. After centrifuging, the supernatant can either be poured off into a second test tube or removed with a pipet. Remember that in most cases both the precipitate and the supernatant must be carried through subsequent steps. Carefully label all test tubes to avoid confusion. Wash precipitates once with distilled water before proceeding to the next step; the rinse water may be discarded.

- When centrifuging test tubes, it is important to keep the centrifuge (rotor) balanced. Do this by arranging test tubes symmetrically in the centrifuge. Never fill a test tube to capacity when placing it in the centrifuge. Leave at least 1 cm free space above the liquid level. Fill all test tubes to the same height before placing them in the centrifuge.

*Teacher Notes*

## Procedure

1. Read the *Materials* section, the *General Techniques for Qualitative Analysis,* and the recommended *Safety Precautions*.

2. Write a detailed, step-by-step procedure for the parallel qualitative analysis of known and unknown solutions containing iron(III), silver, and zinc ions. Include all necessary safety precautions.

3. Construct a suitable data table(s) for recording observations and results.

4. Verify the procedure and data table(s) with your instructor and review all safety precautions.

5. Carry out the experiment and record observations. *Note:* Reference solutions of the individual metal cations will be provided to test the reactions of each metal cation with each reagent, if desired. These optional reference tests may be helpful in deciding how much of a precipitating or complex-forming agent should be added to achieve a desired outcome.

*It is essential that the teacher review the safety precautions with the students before they begin work in the lab. The teacher may decide not to "correct" the procedure itself, preferring instead to let students learn by trial and error (see the Lab Hints). This is up to the teacher's discretion. Do not, however, allow students to proceed with any unsafe steps or without a thorough understanding of the potential safety hazards.*

*Page 5 –* **Chemical Reactions and Qualitative Analysis**

Teacher Notes

**Post-Lab Questions**

1. What cation(s) are present in the unknown sample? How do you know?

2. Write a *net ionic equation* for each of the following steps in the qualitative analysis scheme.

    (a) Separation of silver ions, $Ag^+$

    (b) Confirmation of silver ions, $Ag^+$

    (c) Separation of iron(III) ions, $Fe^{3+}$

    (d) Confirmation of iron(III) ions, $Fe^{3+}$

    (e) Confirmation of zinc ions, $Zn^{2+}$

3. Why is it necessary to use excess sodium hydroxide solution when separating iron(III) and zinc ions?

4. Precipitation reactions are also used in quantitative analysis to determine the precise amount of a metal cation in solution. The most common method for the analysis of barium ions, for example, involves precipitation with sodium sulfate to form barium sulfate, which is insoluble in water.

    (a) Write a molecular equation and a net ionic equation for the precipitation reaction of barium chloride with sodium sulfate.

    (b) What volume of 0.1 M sodium sulfate solution must be added to a water sample containing 0.50 g of dissolved barium ions to ensure that all of the barium precipitates as barium sulfate?

Chemical Reactions and Qualitative Analysis

# Teacher's Notes
## Chemical Reactions and Qualitative Analysis

*Teacher Notes*

**Master Materials List** *(for a class of 30 students working in pairs)*

"Known" samples for qualitative analysis, 50 mL
  Mixture of Fe(NO$_3$)$_3$, AgNO$_3$, and Zn(NO$_3$)$_2$ (0.05 M in each cation)

Reference samples for qualitative analysis (optional)
  Iron(III) nitrate, Fe(NO$_3$)$_3$, 0.05 M, 50 mL
  Silver nitrate, AgNO$_3$, 0.05 M, 50 mL
  Zinc nitrate, Zn(NO$_3$)$_2$, 0.05 M, 50 mL

"Unknown" samples for qualitative analysis, 3 mL for each group
  (see the *Preparation of Solutions* section)

Ammonia (ammonium hydroxide) solution, NH$_3$, 6 M, 50 mL

Hydrochloric acid, HCl, 3 M, 50 mL

Sodium hydroxide solution, NaOH, 6 M, 50 mL

Potassium ferrocyanide solution, K$_4$Fe(CN)$_6$, 0.2 M, 25 mL

Potassium thiocyanate solution, KSCN, 0.2 M, 25 mL

Centrifuge

Litmus paper

Pipets, Beral-type, 150

Reaction plates, 24-well, 15 (optional)

Stirring rods, 15

Stoppers, size 00 (to fit test tubes), 30

Test tubes, 13 × 100 mm, 90

Test tube racks, 15

Water, distilled, and wash bottles, 15

Wax pencils or permanent markers, 15

**Preparation of Solutions** *(for two classes of 30 students working in pairs)*

*Iron(III) Nitrate, 0.15 M Stock Solution:* Add 6.0 g of iron(III) nitrate dodecahydrate [Fe(NO$_3$)$_3$·9H$_2$O] to about 50 mL of distilled or deionized water and stir to dissolve. Dilute to 100 mL with water. *Note:* To prepare 50 mL of the 0.05 M reference solution, dilute 16.7 mL of the stock solution to 50 mL with water.

*Silver Nitrate, 0.15 M Stock Solution:* Add 2.5 g of silver nitrate to about 50 mL of distilled or deionized water and stir to dissolve. Dilute to 100 mL with water. *Note:* To prepare 50 mL of the 0.05 M reference solution, dilute 16.7 mL of the stock solution to 50 mL with water.

*Zinc Nitrate, 0.15 M Stock Solution:* Add 4.5 g of zinc nitrate hexahydrate [Zn(NO$_3$)$_2$·6H$_2$O] to about 50 mL of distilled or deionized water and stir to dissolve. Dilute to 100 mL with water. *Note:* To prepare 50 mL of the 0.05 M reference solution, dilute 16.7 mL of the stock solution to 50 mL with water.

*Potassium ferrocyanide, K$_4$Fe(CN)$_6$, is also known as potassium hexacyanoferrate(II).*

# Teacher's Notes

*"Known" Sample for Qualitative Analysis:* Mix 33.3 mL of the three metal nitrate stock solutions (see above) to prepare 100 mL of a known sample containing 0.05 M of each metal.

*"Unknown" Samples for Qualitative Analysis:* Prepare about 25 mL each of six different unknowns (three individual metal nitrates plus three different possible combinations of two metal nitrates, e.g., iron(III) nitrate/silver nitrate, iron(III) nitrate/zinc nitrate, and silver nitrate/zinc nitrate). Randomly distribute the six possible unknowns among 30 labeled vials to give each student group a unique unknown.

| Unknown | Preparation from 0.15 M Stock Solution |
|---|---|
| 0.05 M $Ag^+$ | Dilute 8.3 mL $AgNO_3$(aq) to 25 mL. |
| 0.05 M $Fe^{3+}$ | Dilute 8.3 mL $Fe(NO_3)_3$(aq) to 25 mL. |
| 0.05 M $Zn^{2+}$ | Dilute 8.3 mL $Zn(NO_3)_2$(aq) to 25 mL. |
| 0.05 M $Ag^+$<br>0.05 M $Zn^{2+}$ | Combine 8.3 mL $AgNO_3$(aq) and 8.3 mL $Zn(NO_3)_2$(aq), dilute to 25 mL. |
| 0.05 M $Ag^+$<br>0.05 M $Fe^{3+}$ | Combine 8.3 mL $AgNO_3$(aq) and 8.3 mL $Fe(NO_3)_3$(aq), dilute to 25 mL. |
| 0.05 M $Zn^{2+}$<br>0.05 M $Fe^{3+}$ | Combine 8.3 mL $Zn(NO_3)_2$(aq) and 8.3 mL $Fe(NO_3)_3$(aq), dilute to 25 mL. |

*Ammonia, 6 M:* Using an ice bath, cool about 25 mL of distilled or deionized water. Carefully add 40.5 mL of concentrated (14.8 M) ammonium hydroxide solution and stir to mix. Allow the solution to warm to room temperature and dilute to 100 mL with water.

*Hydrochloric Acid, 3 M:* Carefully add 25 mL of concentrated (12 M) hydrochloric acid to about 50 mL of distilled or deionized water. Stir to mix, then dilute to 100 mL with water. *Note:* Always add acid to water.

*Potassium Ferrocyanide, 0.2 M:* Dissolve 4.2 g of potassium ferrocyanide trihydrate [$K_4Fe(CN)_6 \cdot 3H_2O$] in 50 mL of distilled or deionized water.

*Potassium Thiocyanate, 0.2 M:* Dissolve 0.97 g of potassium thiocyanate (KSCN) in 50 mL of distilled or deionized water.

## Safety Precautions

*Sodium hydroxide and ammonia solutions are corrosive liquids and especially dangerous to the eyes; skin burns are possible. Ammonia is also toxic by inhalation. Hydrochloric acid is toxic by ingestion and inhalation and is corrosive to skin and eyes. Silver nitrate solution is a skin and eye irritant and is slightly toxic by ingestion; iron(III) nitrate solution may also be irritating to body tissues. Potassium ferrocyanide and potassium thiocyanate solutions are slightly toxic by ingestion and may liberate toxic hydrogen cyanide gas upon contact with concentrated acids. Avoid contact of all chemicals with eyes and skin. Keep sodium carbonate and citric acid on hand to clean up acid and base spills, respectively. Wear chemical splash goggles and chemical-resistant gloves and apron. Please consult current Material Safety Data Sheets for additional safety, handling, and disposal information. Remind students to wash their hands thoroughly with soap and water before leaving the lab.*

Chemical Reactions and Qualitative Analysis

**Teacher's Notes**

## Disposal

Consult your current *Flinn Scientific Catalog/Reference Manual* for general guidelines and specific procedures governing the disposal of laboratory waste. Excess sodium hydroxide and ammonium hydroxide may be neutralized with acid and disposed of according to Flinn Suggested Disposal Method #10. Excess hydrochloric acid may be neutralized with base and disposed of according to Flinn Suggested Disposal Method #24b. The reaction mixtures may be washed down the drain with plenty of excess water according to Flinn Suggested Disposal Method #26b.

## Lab Hints

- For best results, schedule at least two 50-minute laboratory periods for completion of this assignment. The qualitative analysis scheme, with positive identification of each cation, can probably be completed in one 50-minute lab period. Scheduling two lab periods for this activity, however, will allow students time to "get their hands wet" as they gain practical experience of how much precipitating agent to add or what a color test will look like. It may be helpful to allow time during an intervening class period for a discussion of the first day's results.

- Student preparation is the most important element for success in a student-directed, inquiry-based activity. The *Pre-Lab Questions* may be assigned to help students plan their tests and to lead a class discussion before students begin work in the lab. To ensure a safe lab environment, it is essential that the teacher check students' procedures and their understanding of the necessary *Safety Precautions,* as recommended in the *Procedure*.

- The precipitation reactions used to separate silver and iron(III) ions were introduced in a previous experiment, "Double Replacement Reactions and Solubility," in this lab manual. If the previous experiment was not done, it may be helpful to give students extra time to carry out optional reference tests with known reference samples, as described in the *Procedure* section.

- See pages 59 and 60 for a detailed procedure and complete sample data. The procedure may be used as an alternative student handout, if desired.

## Teaching Tips

- Typically in a qualitative analysis experiment, the objective is to analyze an unknown and get the "right" answer. Getting the right answer is always good, of course, but it should not obscure the broader purposes of this lab. Qualitative analysis, done right, allows students to develop critical thinking and logical reasoning skills. It also helps them apply what they have learned in one context (chemical reactions) for another purpose, in this case, chemical analysis.

- See *An Example of Qualitative Analysis* in the *Supplementary Information* section for an explanation of the principles and design of qualitative analysis. The example illustrates the reactions involved in the separation and identification of copper, lead, and zinc ions and includes a flow chart diagram. This example may be used as additional background material to help students analyze the reactions of iron(III), silver, and zinc ions in this experiment.

Flinn ChemTopic™ Labs — Chemical Reactions

# Teacher's Notes

Teacher Notes

**Answers to Pre-Lab Questions** *(Student answers will vary.)*

1. What precipitation reaction could be used to separate and remove silver ions from a mixture containing iron(III), silver, and zinc ions?

    *Silver ions can be selectively precipitated from a mixture containing iron(III), silver, and zinc ions using hydrochloric acid. Silver chloride (AgCl) will precipitate out as an insoluble white solid and can be separated from the remaining aqueous solution containing soluble $Fe^{3+}$ and $Zn^{2+}$ ions.*

2. What precipitation reaction could be used to separate and remove iron(III) ions from the remaining mixture containing iron(III) and zinc ions?

    *Iron(III) ions can be selectively precipitated from a mixture containing both iron and zinc ions using an excess of sodium hydroxide solution. Iron(III) hydroxide [$Fe(OH)_3$] will precipitate out as a reddish-brown solid and can be separated from the remaining solution of soluble $Zn(OH)_4^{2-}$ complex ions.* **Note to teachers:** *Students will need help with this concept. Stress the importance of adding an excess of sodium hydroxide to prevent the precipitation of $Zn(OH)_2$, which is insoluble in water.*

3. How can the presence of silver ions be positively identified?

    *Silver ions can be positively identified by redissolving the initial silver chloride precipitate using excess ammonia. The resulting complex ion product [$Ag(NH_3)_2^+$] is soluble in water.*

4. How can the presence of iron(III) ions be positively identified?

    *The presence of iron(III) ions can be positively identified by redissolving the $Fe(OH)_3$ precipitate in excess hydrochloric acid and adding potassium thiocyanate, which converts soluble $Fe^{3+}$ ions to characteristic deep red complex ions having the formula $FeSCN^{2+}$.*

5. How can the presence of zinc ions be positively identified?

    *Zinc ions can be positively identified by acidifying the soluble $Zn(OH)_4^{2-}$ ions remaining in solution and precipitating the resulting $Zn^{2+}$ ions with potassium ferrocyanide.*

*Continued on page 58*

Chemical Reactions and Qualitative Analysis

# Teacher's Notes

6. Complete the following flow chart.

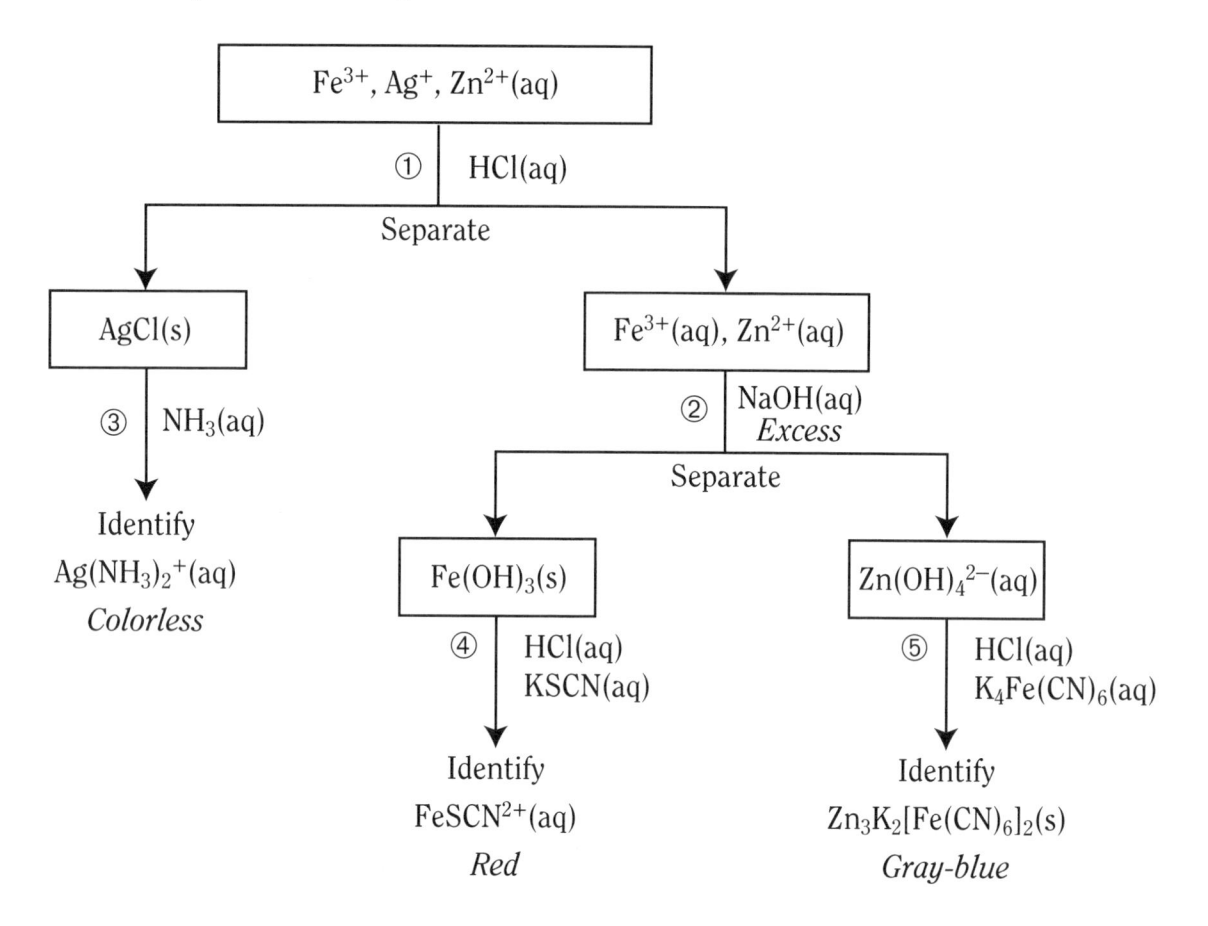

```
                    ┌─────────────────────────┐
                    │  Fe³⁺, Ag⁺, Zn²⁺(aq)    │
                    └───────────┬─────────────┘
                        ①  │  HCl(aq)
                           Separate
              ┌────────────┴────────────┐
              ▼                         ▼
        ┌─────────┐            ┌──────────────────────┐
        │ AgCl(s) │            │  Fe³⁺(aq), Zn²⁺(aq) │
        └────┬────┘            └──────────┬───────────┘
     ③  │ NH₃(aq)                    ②  │ NaOH(aq)
        ▼                                │  Excess
      Identify                       Separate
     Ag(NH₃)₂⁺(aq)          ┌───────────┴───────────┐
      Colorless              ▼                       ▼
                       ┌───────────┐        ┌──────────────┐
                       │ Fe(OH)₃(s)│        │ Zn(OH)₄²⁻(aq)│
                       └─────┬─────┘        └───────┬──────┘
                       ④  │ HCl(aq)          ⑤  │ HCl(aq)
                          │ KSCN(aq)             │ K₄Fe(CN)₆(aq)
                          ▼                      ▼
                       Identify               Identify
                      FeSCN²⁺(aq)          Zn₃K₂[Fe(CN)₆]₂(s)
                          Red                  Gray-blue
```

**Figure 1.** Qualitative Analysis of $Fe^{3+}$, $Ag^+$, and $Zn^{2+}$ Ions.

# Teacher's Notes

Teacher Notes

## Sample Procedure

### Part A. Separation of Metal Ions

1. Label five small test tubes #1–5. Place about 1 mL (20 drops) of the solution to be analyzed into test tube #1. Record the sample identity and the color of the solution in the data table.

2. Add 5 drops of 3 M HCl and stir to mix. Record the appearance and color of any precipitate.

3. Centrifuge the mixture to separate the solid, if necessary.

4. Test to be sure precipitation is complete: Add one more drop of 3 M HCl to the supernatant. If more precipitate appears, continue adding 3 M HCl dropwise until no more solid forms.

5. Centrifuge and decant (pour off) the supernatant into test tube #2. Alternatively, use a Beral-type pipet to remove the supernatant. Record the color and appearance of the solution in the data table.

6. Save the precipitate in test tube #1 for Part B, step 11.

7. Add 5 drops of 6 M NaOH to the solution in test tube #2.

8. Stir the solution and test with litmus paper to be sure the solution is basic, then add 3 more drops of 6 M NaOH. Record the appearance and color of any precipitate.

9. Centrifuge the mixture to separate the solid, if necessary. Decant the supernatant into test tube #3. Alternatively, use a Beral-type pipet to remove the supernatant. Save the precipitate in test tube #2 for use in Part B, step 13.

10. Record the color and appearance of the solution in test tube #3 and save the solution for use in Part B, step 16.

### Part B. Identification of Metal Ions

11. Rinse the precipitate in test tube #1 with 10 drops of distilled water. Tap or swirl the test tube to mix the contents. Centrifuge the mixture and decant the rinse water.

12. Add 8–10 drops of 6 M $NH_3$ to the solid in test tube #1 and stir to mix. Record observations in the data table.

13. Rinse the precipitate in test tube #2 with 10 drops of distilled water. Tap or swirl the test tube to mix the contents. Centrifuge the mixture and decant the rinse water.

14. Add 5–7 drops of 3 M HCl to the solid in test tube #2 and stir to mix. Test the solution with litmus paper to be sure it is acidic. Record observations in the data table.

15. Add 3 drops of 0.2 M KSCN to the solution in test tube #2 and record observations in the data table.

16. Add 8–10 drops of 3 M HCl to the solution in test tube #3 until the solution tests acidic with litmus paper.

17. Add 3 drops of 0.2 M $K_4Fe(CN)_6$ to the resulting acidic solution in test tube #3 and record observations in the data table.

Chemical Reactions and Qualitative Analysis

# Teacher's Notes

## Sample Data Table
*Student data will vary.*

| Sample Identity | "Known" Solution | Color of Solution | Pale yellow |
|---|---|---|---|

**Observations and Results**

| Step | Test Tube | Observations | Conclusions |
|---|---|---|---|
| 2 | 1 | White precipitate forms. | $Ag^+$ ions are present. |
| 5 | 2 | Solution is pale yellow. | NA |
| 8 | 2 | Rust-colored precipitate forms. | $Fe^{3+}$ ions are present. |
| 10 | 3 | Solution is clear and colorless. | NA |
| 12 | 1 | White precipitate dissolves. | Confirms presence of $Ag^+$ ions. |
| 14 | 2 | Red precipitate dissolves to give yellow solution. | NA |
| 15 | 2 | Solution turns deep red. | Confirms presence of $Fe^{3+}$ ions. |
| 17 | 3 | Gray-blue precipitate forms. | Confirms presence of $Zn^{2+}$ ions. |

## Answers to Post-Lab Questions *(Student answers will vary.)*

1. What cation(s) are present in the unknown sample? How do you know?

   ***Note to teachers:*** *For best results, randomly distribute unknowns among students. Students should explain their reasoning for both the presence and absence of specific ions. For example, consider an unknown containing only $Zn^{2+}$ ions. When HCl was added, no precipitate was observed, thus $Ag^+$ ions were not present. Also, no precipitate formed when excess NaOH was added, indicating that $Fe^{3+}$ ions were not present. Finally, adding $K_4Fe(CN)_6$ gave a gray-blue precipitate, confirming that $Zn^{2+}$ ions were present.*

2. Write a *net ionic equation* for each of the following steps in the qualitative analysis scheme.

   (a) Separation of silver ions, $Ag^+$

   $$Ag^+(aq) + Cl^-(aq) \rightarrow AgCl(s)$$

   (b) Confirmation of silver ions, $Ag^+$

   $$AgCl(s) + 2NH_3(aq) \rightarrow Ag(NH_3)_2^+(aq)$$

   (c) Separation of iron(III) ions, $Fe^{3+}$

   $$Fe^{3+}(aq) + 3OH^-(aq) \rightarrow Fe(OH)_3(s)$$

**Teacher Notes**

(d) Confirmation of iron(III) ions, $Fe^{3+}$

$Fe^{3+}(aq) + SCN^-(aq) \rightarrow FeSCN^{2+}(aq)$

(e) Confirmation of zinc ions, $Zn^{2+}$

$3Zn^{2+}(aq) + 2K^+(aq) + 2Fe(CN)_6^{4-}(aq) \rightarrow Zn_3K_2[Fe(CN)_6]_2(s)$

3. Why is it necessary to use excess sodium hydroxide solution when separating iron(III) and zinc ions?

   *Both iron(III) and zinc hydroxide are insoluble in water. Adding excess sodium hydroxide converts $Zn(OH)_2(s)$ to soluble $Zn(OH)_4^{2-}$ complex ions. Only the iron(III) ions will precipitate out when excess sodium hydroxide is used.*

4. Precipitation reactions are also used in quantitative analysis to determine the precise amount of a metal cation in solution. The most common method for the analysis of barium ions, for example, involves precipitation with sodium sulfate to form barium sulfate, which is insoluble in water.

   (a) Write a molecular equation and a net ionic equation for the precipitation reaction of barium chloride with sodium sulfate.

   $BaCl_2(aq) + Na_2SO_4(aq) \rightarrow BaSO_4(s) + 2NaCl(aq)$

   $Ba^{2+}(aq) + SO_4^{2-}(aq) \rightarrow BaSO_4(s)$

   (b) What volume of 0.1 M sodium sulfate solution must be added to a water sample containing 0.50 g of dissolved barium ions to ensure that all of the barium precipitates as barium sulfate?

   *Atomic mass of barium = 137.33 g/mole*

   $0.50 \text{ g } Ba^{2+} \text{ ions} \times \dfrac{1 \text{ mole}}{137.33 \text{ g}} = 0.0036 \text{ moles } Ba^{2+} \text{ ions}$

   $0.0036 \text{ moles } Ba^{2+} \text{ ions} \times \dfrac{1 \text{ mole } Na_2SO_4}{1 \text{ mole } Ba^{2+}} = 0.0036 \text{ moles } Na_2SO_4$

   $0.0036 \text{ moles } Na_2SO_4 \times \dfrac{1 \text{ liter}}{0.1 \text{ moles}} = 0.036 \text{ L } (36 \text{ mL}) \text{ of } 0.1 \text{ M } Na_2SO_4$

**Teacher's Notes**

## Supplementary Information

### *An Example of Qualitative Analysis*

### *Separation and Identification of Copper, Lead, and Zinc Ions*

Copper ($Cu^{2+}$), lead ($Pb^{2+}$), and zinc ($Zn^{2+}$) ions may be naturally present in water due to erosion of rock and soil. Elevated levels of these cations may also arise due to corrosion of plumbing systems and industrial pipes. One possible qualitative analysis scheme for the separation and identification of $Cu^{2+}$, $Pb^{2+}$, and $Zn^{2+}$ ions in water is shown in Figure 1.

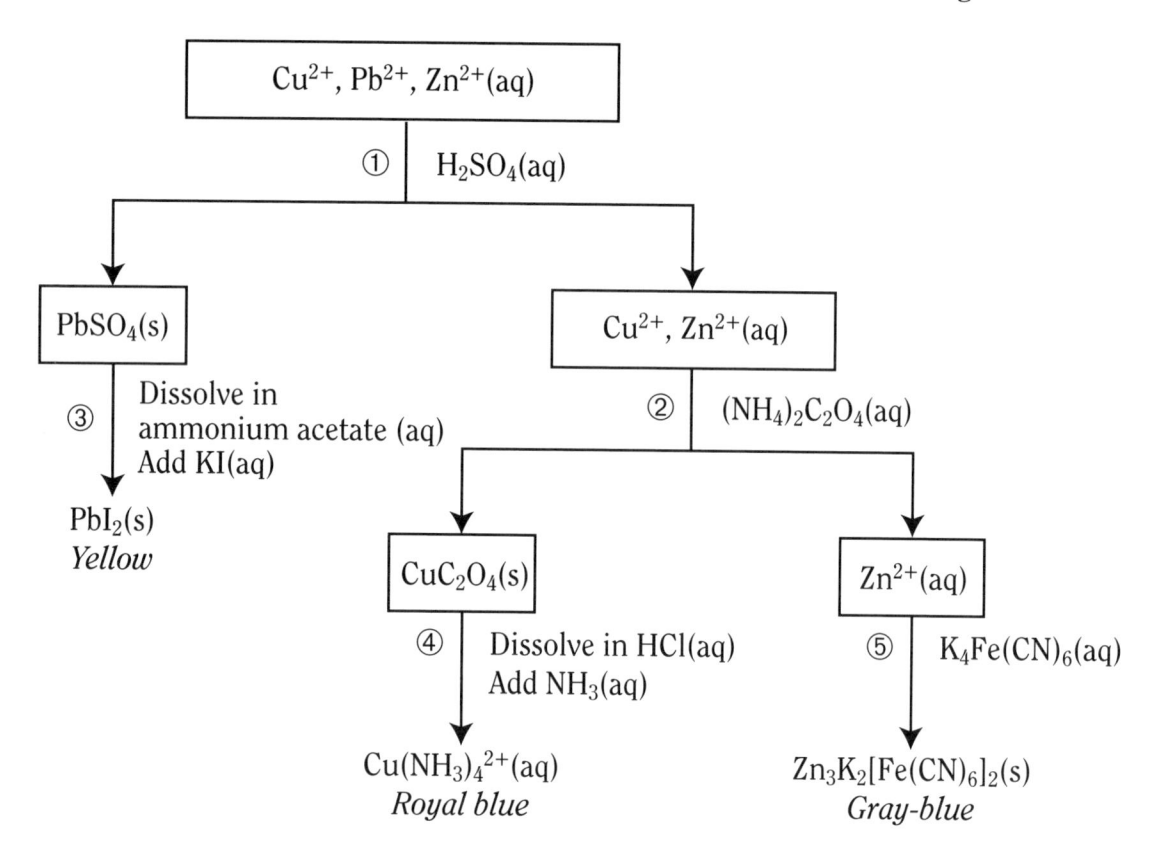

```
            ┌─────────────────────────┐
            │ Cu²⁺, Pb²⁺, Zn²⁺ (aq)   │
            └───────────┬─────────────┘
                    ① │ H₂SO₄(aq)
         ┌─────────────┴─────────────┐
         ▼                           ▼
   ┌──────────┐              ┌────────────────┐
   │ PbSO₄(s) │              │ Cu²⁺, Zn²⁺(aq) │
   └────┬─────┘              └────────┬───────┘
        │ Dissolve in          ② │ (NH₄)₂C₂O₄(aq)
     ③  │ ammonium acetate (aq)   │
        │ Add KI(aq)         ┌────┴────┐
        ▼                    ▼         ▼
     PbI₂(s)           ┌─────────┐  ┌────────┐
     Yellow            │ CuC₂O₄(s)│ │Zn²⁺(aq)│
                       └────┬────┘  └───┬────┘
                         ④ │ Dissolve   │ ⑤ K₄Fe(CN)₆(aq)
                            │ in HCl(aq)│
                            │ Add NH₃(aq)│
                            ▼            ▼
                     Cu(NH₃)₄²⁺(aq)   Zn₃K₂[Fe(CN)₆]₂(s)
                      Royal blue         Gray-blue
```

**Figure 1.** Qualitative Analysis Scheme for $Cu^{2+}$, $Pb^{2+}$, and $Zn^{2+}$ Ions.

Separation of the individual cations from the mixture is based on the following chemical reactions:

(1) Selective precipitation of lead sulfate ($PbSO_4$) using sulfuric acid (Equations 1a–c).

$$Pb^{2+}(aq) + H_2SO_4(aq) \rightarrow PbSO_4(s) + 2H^+(aq) \quad \textit{Equation 1a}$$

$$Cu^{2+}(aq) + H_2SO_4(aq) \rightarrow \text{No Reaction} \quad \textit{Equation 1b}$$

$$Zn^{2+}(aq) + H_2SO_4(aq) \rightarrow \text{No Reaction} \quad \textit{Equation 1c}$$

**Teacher Notes**

(2) Precipitation of copper oxalate (CuC$_2$O$_4$) from the remaining solution using ammonium oxalate (Equations 2a and 2b).

$$Cu^{2+}(aq) + (NH_4)_2C_2O_4 \rightarrow CuC_2O_4(s) + 2NH_4^+(aq) \qquad \textit{Equation 2a}$$
Blue

$$Zn^{2+}(aq) + (NH_4)_2C_2O_4 \rightarrow \text{No Reaction} \qquad \textit{Equation 2b}$$

Subsequent chemical reactions allow for positive identification of each individual cation:

(3) The PbSO$_4$(s) precipitate can be redissolved in ammonium acetate (NH$_4$C$_2$H$_3$O$_2$) solution and the resulting Pb$^{2+}$ ions converted to lead iodide, a characteristic yellow solid (Equations 3a and 3b).

$$PbSO_4(s) + 2NH_4C_2H_3O_2(aq) \rightarrow Pb(C_2H_3O_2)_2(aq) + (NH_4)_2SO_4(aq) \qquad \textit{Equation 3a}$$

$$Pb^{2+}(aq) + 2KI(aq) \rightarrow PbI_2(s) + 2K^+(aq) \qquad \textit{Equation 3b}$$
Yellow

(4) The CuC$_2$O$_4$(s) precipitate can be redissolved with hydrochloric acid and the resulting Cu$^{2+}$ ions converted to characteristic, royal blue complex ions Cu(NH$_3$)$_4^{2+}$ by adding ammonia (Equations 4a and 4b).

$$CuC_2O_4(s) + 2HCl(aq) \rightarrow CuCl_2(aq) + H_2C_2O_4(aq) \qquad \textit{Equation 4a}$$

$$Cu^{2+}(aq) + 4NH_3(aq) \rightarrow Cu(NH_3)_4^{2+}(aq) \qquad \textit{Equation 4b}$$
Royal blue

(5) The remaining Zn(OH)$_4^{2-}$(aq) solution can be acidified with HCl and the zinc ions can then be precipitated as Zn$_3$K$_2$[Fe(CN)$_6$]$_2$, a characteristic gray-blue solid, by adding potassium ferrocyanide [K$_4$Fe(CN)$_6$] (Equations 5a and 5b).

$$Zn(OH)_4^{2-}(aq) + 4HCl(aq) \rightarrow Zn^{2+}(aq) + 4H_2O(l) + 4Cl^-(aq) \qquad \textit{Equation 5a}$$

$$3Zn^{2+}(aq) + 2K_4Fe(CN)_6(aq) \rightarrow Zn_3K_2[Fe(CN)_6]_2(s) + 6K^+(aq) \qquad \textit{Equation 5b}$$
Gray–blue

# Teacher's Notes

# Demonstrations

**Teacher Notes**

# Chemical Reactions Primer
## Observation and Classification

## Introduction

Chemical reactions are the lifeblood of chemistry. Recognizing chemical reactions and "translating" them into chemical equations are essential skills that students must develop in order to be successful in chemistry. Use the following activity to give students extra practice observing and classifying chemical reactions or to assess student understanding of the five basic types of reactions.

## Concepts

- Chemical reactions
- Single vs. double replacement
- Combination vs. decomposition
- Combustion reactions

## Materials

Ammonia (ammonium hydroxide), 6 M, $NH_3$, 5 mL
Bromcresol green solution, 0.04% aqueous, 1 mL
Copper(II) chloride solution, 1 M, $CuCl_2$, 15 mL
Ethyl alcohol, $C_2H_5OH$, 1 mL
Hydrochloric acid, 3 M, HCl, 10 mL
Hydrogen peroxide solution, 6%, $H_2O_2$, 5 mL
Iron(III) chloride solution, 1 M, $FeCl_3$, 5 mL
Iron wire, Fe, 4–5 cm
Phenol red solution, 0.02% aqueous, 1 mL
Sodium hydroxide solution, 1 M, NaOH, 5 mL
Sodium phosphate solution, 0.5 M, $Na_3PO_4$, 5 mL
Sulfur powder, S, 0.1 g
Sulfuric acid, 1 M, $H_2SO_4$, 2 mL
Yeast, Baker's, 0.3 g
Zinc, mossy, Zn, 5–6 small pieces

Bunsen burner
Butane safety lighter
Deflagration spoon
Distilled water
Erlenmeyer flask, 250-mL
Evaporating dish, porcelain
Graduated cylinders, 10-mL, 5
Heat-resistant pad
Pipets, Beral-type, 5
Spatula
Test tubes, 16 × 150 mm, 7
Test tube clamp
Test tube rack
Wood splints, 2

*Copper(II) chloride is also called cupric chloride and iron(III) chloride is also known as ferric chloride. The sodium phosphate solution required for this activity is prepared from sodium phosphate, tribasic ($Na_3PO_4$), which is sometimes called trisodium phosphate.*

## Safety Precautions

*Ethyl alcohol is a flammable solvent and a dangerous fire risk. Keep away from flames and other sources of ignition. Solvent bottles should be kept capped at all times and must be removed from the work area when using the laboratory burner. Concentrated ammonia solution is extremely corrosive and toxic by inhalation. Ammonia vapors are extremely irritating to the eyes and respiratory tract. Sulfuric acid, hydrochloric acid, and sodium hydroxide solutions are corrosive liquids. Keep sodium carbonate and citric acid on hand to clean up acid and base spills, respectively. Hydrogen peroxide solution is a strong oxidizing agent and is corrosive to skin, eyes, and the respiratory tract. Sulfur powder is flammable and zinc metal may also contain a flammable dust. Burning sulfur generates sulfur dioxide, a toxic gas with a stinging, irritating odor. Work with burning sulfur in the hood or in a*

# Demonstrations

*well-ventilated lab only. Copper(II) chloride solution is slightly toxic by ingestion. Iron(III) chloride and sodium phosphate solutions may be irritating to the eyes and skin. Avoid contact of all chemicals with eyes and skin. Wear chemical splash goggles and chemical-resistant gloves and apron. Please review current Material Safety Data Sheets for additional safety, handling, and disposal information.*

## Procedure

Record the color and appearance of the reactant(s), the evidence for the chemical reaction, and the properties of the product(s).

### Reaction #1

1. Measure 50 mL of distilled water into a 250-mL Erlenmeyer flask and add about 10 drops of bromcresol green indicator. The water will be green or blue at this point.

2. Fill a deflagration spoon about ¼-full with powdered sulfur. *Caution:* Carry out steps 3–5 in a fume hood or a well-ventilated lab only.

3. Heat the spoon in a laboratory burner flame until the sulfur melts, turns red, and starts to burn.

4. Holding the deflagration spoon upright, lower the spoon into the 250-mL Erlenmeyer flask until the spoon rests about 1–2 cm above the water surface in the flask. Do NOT allow the spoon to touch the water.

5. Observe the resulting color change in the indicator solution as the gaseous reaction product(s) dissolves in water.

### Reaction #2

6. Using a graduated cylinder, add about 10 mL of 1 M copper(II) chloride solution into a large test tube.

7. Loosely coil a 4–5 cm piece of iron wire. Add the wire to the test tube and observe the resulting chemical reaction.

### Reaction #3

8. Using a graduated cylinder, add about 5 mL of 1 M copper(II) chloride solution into a large test tube.

9. Using a clean graduated cylinder, add about 5 mL of 6 M ammonia (ammonium hydroxide) solution to the test tube.

### Reaction #4

10. Using a graduated cylinder, measure about 10 mL of 3 M hydrochloric acid solution into a large test tube.

11. Add 5–6 pieces of mossy zinc to the acid in the test tube.

12. Feel the sides of the test tube and observe the resulting chemical reaction for one minute.

13. Light a wood splint and quickly place the burning splint in the mouth of the test tube. Do not put the burning splint into the acid solution.

---

**Teacher Notes**

*Ask students to set up a data table to record observations and help them interpret the reactions when the activity is over.*

# Demonstrations

**Teacher Notes**

### Reaction #5

14. Using a graduated cylinder, add about 5 mL of 1 M iron(III) chloride solution into a large test tube.

15. Slowly add 10 mL of 0.5 M sodium phosphate solution to the test tube.

### Reaction #6

16. Measure about 0.3 g of solid Baker's yeast into a large test tube.

17. Add about 5 mL of 6% hydrogen peroxide solution and observe the resulting chemical reaction.

18. Test for the formation of a gas: Insert a glowing (not burning) wood splint about halfway down the test tube. Do not allow the glowing splint to contact the liquid.

### Reaction #7

19. Using a Beral-type pipet, add 40 drops of 1 M sulfuric acid solution to a large test tube.

20. Add 2 mL of distilled water, followed by 5 drops of phenol red indicator, to the test tube. Mix the solution by gently swirling the test tube.

21. Using a clean, Beral-type pipet, add 1 M sodium hydroxide solution one drop at a time to the test tube. Count the number of drops of base required for a permanent color change to be observed.

### Reaction #8

22. Working in the hood or a designated work area, add about 1 mL (20 drops) of ethyl alcohol to a clean evaporating dish. Place the evaporating dish on a heat-resistant pad.

23. Cap the alcohol bottle and remove it from the work area.

24. Light a butane safety lighter and bring the flame close to the alcohol in the evaporating dish.

25. Turn off the safety lighter as soon as the alcohol ignites.

26. Fill a test tube about one-third full with cold tap water. Place the test tube in a test tube clamp and hold the test tube above the burning alcohol flames.

27. Allow the alcohol to burn until it is completely consumed. *Caution:* Do not touch the hot evaporating dish.

## Disposal

Consult your current *Flinn Scientific Catalog/Reference Manual* for general guidelines and specific procedures governing the disposal of laboratory waste. Excess sodium hydroxide and ammonium hydroxide may be neutralized with acid and disposed of according to Flinn Suggested Disposal Method #10. Excess hydrochloric acid and sulfuric acid may be neutralized with base and disposed of according to Flinn Suggested Disposal Method #24b. The mixture resulting from Reaction #2 contains solid iron which will clog the drains if discarded in the

*Reactions #2, 3, 5, and 6 can be safely scaled up for better viewing, if desired.*

# Demonstrations

sink. Pour this mixture onto several pairs of thickly folded paper towels and discard in the trash according to Flinn Suggested Disposal Method #26a. All other reaction mixtures may be washed down the drain with plenty of excess water according to Flinn Suggested Disposal Method #26b.

## Tips

- This activity is written as a demonstration but may be presented in a variety of ways. The reactions may be performed in conjunction with the experiment "Classifying Chemical Reactions" to introduce the topic and provide extra practice observing and classifying chemical reactions. The demonstration may also be used by the instructor as an assessment tool to test the students' ability to predict the products of chemical reactions and to write balanced chemical equations.

- The sequence of reactions has been arranged in random fashion with respect to the type of reaction. Depending on how the demonstration is used, however, it may be helpful to organize the reactions by reaction type (see the *Discussion* section).

## Discussion

Chemical reactions may be classified based on the number of reactants and products, their physical and chemical nature, and the rearrangement of atoms in the conversion of reactants into products. See Table 1 for descriptions and examples of five common types of reactions.

## Table 1. Classification of Chemical Reactions

| Type of Reaction | General Description and Example(s) |
| --- | --- |
| Combination | Two reactants combine to form a single product. The reactants may be elements or compounds. Also called a synthesis reaction. <br> $Zn(s) + I_2(s) \rightarrow ZnI_2(s)$ <br> $CaO(s) + H_2O(l) \rightarrow Ca(OH)_2(s)$ |
| Decomposition | One reactant, a compound, breaks down to give two or more products. <br> $2H_2O_2(aq) \rightarrow 2H_2O(l) + O_2(g)$ |
| Single Replacement | An element reacts with a compound and replaces one of the elements in the compound. Metals replace hydrogen or other metals; nonmetals replace nonmetals. <br> $Zn(s) + 2HCl(aq) \rightarrow H_2(g) + ZnCl_2(aq)$ <br> $Cu(s) + 2AgNO_3(aq) \rightarrow 2Ag(s) + Cu(NO_3)_2(aq)$ <br> $Cl_2(aq) + 2NaI(aq) \rightarrow I_2(aq) + 2NaCl(aq)$ |
| Double Replacement | Two ionic compounds (or compounds that break apart to form ions in solution) exchange ions to form new compounds. Examples include precipitation reactions (driving force is formation of a precipitate), acid–base reactions (driving force is formation of water), and gas-forming reactions (driving force is evolution of a gas). <br> $NaCl(aq) + AgNO_3(aq) \rightarrow AgCl(s) + NaNO_3(aq)$ <br> $H_2SO_4(aq) + 2NaOH(aq) \rightarrow Na_2SO_4(aq) + 2H_2O(l)$ <br> $Na_2SO_3(aq) + 2HCl(aq) \rightarrow 2NaCl(aq) + H_2O(l) + SO_2(g)$ |
| Combustion | A compound burns in the presence of oxygen, producing energy in the form of heat and light. The combustion of organic compounds produces carbon dioxide and water. <br> $C_4H_8(l) + 6O_2(g) \rightarrow 4CO_2(g) + 4H_2O(g)$ |

# Demonstrations

**Teacher Notes**

## Results

Write a balanced chemical equation for each reaction #1–8 and classify each reaction.

Reaction #1: $S(s) + O_2(g) \xrightarrow{\Delta} SO_2(g)$
$SO_2(g) + H_2O(l) \rightarrow H_2SO_3(aq)$
$H_2SO_3(aq) \rightarrow H^+(aq) + HSO_3^-(aq)$
*Combination reactions and acid–base reaction*

Reaction #2: $2Fe(s) + 3CuCl_2(aq) \rightarrow 2FeCl_3(aq) + 3Cu(s)$
*Single-replacement reaction*

Reaction #3: $CuCl_2(aq) + 4NH_3(aq) \rightarrow Cu(NH_3)_4Cl_2(aq)$
*Combination (complex-ion forming) reaction*

Reaction #4: $Zn(s) + 2HCl(aq) \rightarrow ZnCl_2(aq) + H_2(g)$
*Single-replacement reaction*

Reaction #5: $FeCl_3(aq) + Na_3PO_4(aq) \rightarrow FePO_4(s) + 3NaCl(aq)$
*Double-replacement reaction*

Reaction #6: $2H_2O_2(aq) \xrightarrow{Yeast} 2H_2O(l) + O_2(g)$
*Decomposition reaction*

Reaction #7: $H_2SO_4(aq) + 2NaOH \rightarrow Na_2SO_4(aq) + 2H_2O(l)$
*Double-replacement reaction*

Reaction #8: $C_2H_6O(g) + 3O_2(g) \xrightarrow{\Delta} 2CO_2(g) + 3H_2O(g)$
*Combustion reaction*

Chemical Reactions Primer

# Demonstrations

# Colorful Electrolysis
## Decomposition of Water

Teacher Notes

## Introduction

Demonstrate the electrolysis of water in simple but colorful fashion on an overhead projector.

## Concepts

- Decomposition reaction
- Electrolysis
- Oxidation–reduction

## Materials

Petri dish with cover
Battery clip with alligator ends
Battery, 9-V
Universal indicator solution, 100 mL
Universal Indicator Overhead Color Chart (optional)

Sodium chloride, NaCl, 20 g
Beaker, 1-L
Distilled water, 500 mL
Overhead projector
Stirring rod

## Safety Precautions

*Universal indicator is an alcohol-based solution and is flammable; do not use near an open flame. Wear chemical splash goggles and chemical-resistant gloves and apron. Please review current Material Safety Data Sheets for additional safety, handling, and disposal information.*

## Preparation

Prepare the electrolysis solution by mixing 100 mL of universal indicator solution and 500 mL distilled water with 20 g of sodium chloride in a 1-L beaker.

Stir until the sodium chloride dissolves. Store the solution in a capped container until ready to use. For best results, prepare the solution the day of the demonstration. *Note:* This volume of solution (600 mL) is enough to carry out the demonstration as written seven times. If less than 600 mL of solution is needed, decrease the amounts proportionately.

## Procedure

1. Place the top and bottom halves of a Petri dish on the projection stage of an overhead projector.

2. Pour enough electrolysis solution into each half of the Petri dish to just cover the bottom. Adjust the overhead so that the dishes are in clear focus. Each half dish should appear to be a rich, transparent green color.

3. Attach the alligator clips of the battery clip over the edges of the Petri dish top. Place the clips at opposite sides of the dish as shown in Figure 1. The ends of the alligator clips should be submerged in the green electrolysis solution.

*"Colorful Electrolysis" is available as a Chemical Demonstration Kit from Flinn Scientific (Catalog No. AP6467).*

Flinn ChemTopic™ Labs — Chemical Reactions

## Demonstrations

**Teacher Notes**

4. To start the demonstration, clip the 9-volt battery into the snaps on the battery clip. See Figure 1.

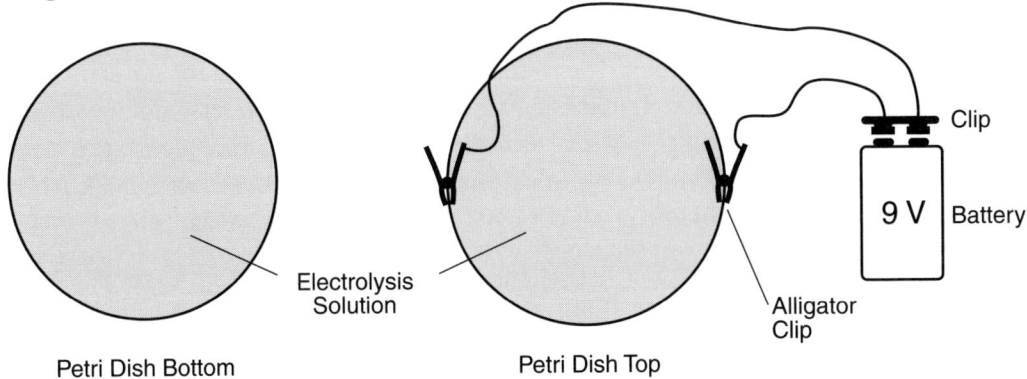

**Figure 1.** Demonstration Setup.

5. Let the demonstration proceed for 5–10 minutes and note the changing colors over time. *(A purple color will appear at the negative electrode very quickly. An orange color will develop more slowly at the positive electrode. Over time, the entire spectrum of universal indicator colors will appear.)*

6. Observe the production of gas bubbles at the electrodes. *(Hydrogen gas is produced at the negative electrode, oxygen gas at the positive electrode. The bubbling will appear more rapid at the negative electrode, because two moles of hydrogen are produced per mole of oxygen.)*

7. Discuss the results as the demonstration continues. Analyze the various colors that are produced as well as why the "extra" dish was included in the demonstration.

### Disposal

Please consult your current *Flinn Scientific Catalog/Reference Manual* for general guidelines and specific procedures concerning the disposal of laboratory wastes. The electrolysis solution may be disposed of according to Flinn Suggested Disposal Method #26b.

### Tips

- Concepts of pH and electrolysis should be discussed prior to the demonstration. Universal indicator colors, as they relate to pH values, should also be discussed. The Universal Indicator Overhead Color Chart (Catalog No. AP5367) provides a nice visual supplement during this discussion.

- The demonstration may be repeated using a pH 7 buffer to show the effect of buffering. *(When the solution is buffered, no color changes result.)*

- Try the same demonstration using potassium iodide solution in the Petri dish as follows: 20 g potassium iodide, 500 mL distilled water, and 30 drops phenolphthlein. When potassium iodide is used as the electrolyte in aqueous solution, electrolysis produces iodine at the anode and hydrogen gas at the cathode. The phenolphthalein indicator will turn pink at the cathode due to the formation of $OH^-$ ions.

Colorful Electrolysis

# Demonstrations

## Discussion

When an electric current is passed through an aqueous solution containing an electrolyte (NaCl), the water molecules break apart or decompose into their constituent elements, hydrogen and oxygen. The overall reaction occurs as two separate, independent half-reactions. Reduction of the hydrogen atoms in water to elemental hydrogen ($H_2$) occurs at the cathode (the negative electrode), while oxidation of the oxygen atoms in water to elemental oxygen ($O_2$) occurs at the anode (the positive electrode). Each half-reaction is accompanied by the production of $OH^-$ or $H^+$ ions as shown below:

$$\text{Cathode: } 4e^- + 4H_2O \rightarrow 2H_2(g) + 4OH^- \qquad \textit{Reduction}$$

$$\text{Anode: } 2H_2O \rightarrow O_2(g) + 4H^+ + 4e^- \qquad \textit{Oxidation}$$

The excess $OH^-$ ions produced at the cathode will cause the pH to increase, resulting in a color change of the universal indicator solution from green (neutral, pH 7) to purple (basic, pH ≥10).

The excess $H^+$ ions produced at the anode will cause the pH to decrease, resulting in a color change of the universal indicator solution from green to orange-red (acidic, pH ≤4).

The electrolysis half-reactions can also be followed by observing the production of gas bubbles at the cathode ($H_2$) and anode ($O_2$).

The overall reaction in the electrolysis of water is the decomposition of water, Equation 1.

$$2H_2O(l) \rightarrow 2H_2(g) + O_2(g) \qquad \textit{Equation 1}$$

Universal indicator is an acid–base indicator that is different colors at different pH values. All colors will be visible in the Petri dish as electrolysis progresses and as the pH conditions continually change due to diffusion and neutralization.

| pH | Color |
| --- | --- |
| 4 | Red |
| 5 | Orange |
| 6 | Yellow |
| 7 | Green |
| 8 | Blue-green |
| 9 | Dark blue |
| 10 | Purple |

Teacher Notes

**Teacher Notes**

# The Chef
## A Chemical Reaction That Really Cooks

### Introduction

When water is added to calcium oxide, the amount of heat produced is enough to fry an egg. This is an ideal demonstration to use when discussing exothermic reactions and heats of reaction, but it is also a fun attention-getter that may be used to introduce different types of reactions.

### Concepts

- Combination reaction
- Exothermic reaction

### Materials

Calcium oxide lump, CaO, 200 g (powdered or old calcium oxide will not work)

Water, distilled, 50–100 mL

Cooking oil or Pam® cooking spray

Small aluminum pie pans, 2

Wash bottle for water

Egg, small, 1 (medium or large eggs do not work as well)

Spatula

Chef's hat

Oven mitt or hot pad

### Safety Precautions

*Calcium oxide is a corrosive material and a severe body tissue irritant. Avoid all body tissue contact. Reaction of calcium oxide and water will produce large amounts of heat—skin burns are possible. A lump of calcium oxide may disintegrate violently and splatter when water is added. Wash hands thoroughly when finished. This should be a teacher demonstration only. Do not allow students to perform this procedure. Do not eat the egg after it is cooked. Wear chemical splash goggles and chemical-resistant gloves and apron. Please review current Material Safety Data Sheets for additional safety information.*

### Procedure

1. Place about 200 g of fresh calcium oxide lumps into one of the aluminum pans. The amount needed depends on the size of the lumps. The calcium oxide should form a single, tightly-packed layer on the bottom of the pan.

2. Add 50–100 mL of water to the calcium oxide (a little practice will help determine the right amount of water). Use a wash bottle to distribute the water evenly over the surface. *Warning:* The CaO lumps may splatter—wear goggles and gloves.

3. Add a small amount of cooking oil or Pam to the second pan and place the pan directly on top of the calcium oxide/water mixture.

4. When the second pan and cooking oil are hot, break open a small egg into the top pan.

5. Cook the egg to order.

*"The Chef" is available as a Chemical Demonstration Kit from Flinn Scientific (Catalog No. AP6468).*

# Demonstrations

Teacher Notes

## Disposal

Please consult your current *Flinn Scientific Catalog/Reference Manual* for general guidelines and specific procedures concerning the disposal of laboratory wastes. The calcium hydroxide product remaining in the pan after the demonstration may be diluted with water, neutralized with hydrochloric acid, and then flushed down the drain with excess water according to Flinn Suggested Disposal Method #10.

## Tips

- The shelf life for calcium oxide is poor—always use fresh calcium oxide for best results. Calcium oxide, lump, that is available from Flinn Scientific (Catalog No. C0028) is a special formulation with a low surface area. This reduces the amount of calcium hydroxide present before the water is added. Fresh calcium oxide lump should look like hard pebbles that will crack and become soft when exposed to water.

- Use an oven mitt or hot pad to hold the pans when cooking the egg. Place the aluminum pans on a heat-resistant surface—the bottom pan will get very hot. This reaction generates a lot of heat; use proper care handling the pans.

- A student worksheet is attached for use with this demonstration.

## Discussion

Calcium oxide is also known as lime or quicklime and is used to make plaster, mortar, bricks, and many other construction materials. Calcium oxide is produced by heating limestone (calcium carbonate) in air. However, calcium oxide readily absorbs and reacts with carbon dioxide and water to form calcium carbonate ($CaCO_3$) and calcium hydroxide [$Ca(OH)_2$], respectively. When water is added to calcium oxide, an exothermic reaction occurs, producing calcium hydroxide and a large amount of heat. Calcium hydroxide is used to treat acidic soils, soften water, and prepare building materials such as plaster, mortar, and bricks. The solubility of calcium hydroxide in water is very low, about 1.6 g/L. The product of the reaction of CaO and $H_2O$ is thus $Ca(OH)_2(s)$, not $Ca(OH)_2(aq)$.

$$CaO(s) + H_2O(l) \rightarrow Ca(OH)_2(s) + \text{heat}$$

$$\Delta H = \Delta H_f(\text{products}) - \Delta H_f(\text{reactants})$$

$$\Delta H = \Delta H_f[Ca(OH)_2(s)] - \{\Delta H_f[CaO(s)] + \Delta H_f[H_2O(l)]\}$$

$$\Delta H = -986.1 \text{ kJ/mole} - [-635.1 \text{ kJ/mole} + (-285.8 \text{ kJ/mole})] = -65.2 \text{ kJ/mole}$$

*Special thanks to Dewayne Lieneman, chemistry teacher, Glenbard South High School, Glen Ellyn, Illinois, who provided us with the instructions for this activity.*

Flinn ChemTopic™ Labs — Chemical Reactions

Teacher Notes

Name: _____

Class/Lab Period: _____

# "The Chef" Worksheet

1. Write a balanced chemical equation for the combination reaction of calcium oxide and water to produce calcium hydroxide. *Hint:* If the solubility of calcium hydroxide in water is only 1.6 g/L, what is the state of the major product?

2. Use Hess's Law to express the heat of reaction for this reaction in terms of the heat of formation of the reactants and products.

3. Use the information in the following table to calculate the heat of reaction.

| Chemical | Heat of Formation (kJ/mole) | Molar Mass (g/mole) |
|---|---|---|
| CaO(s) | – 635.1 | 56.08 |
| Ca(OH)$_2$(s) | – 986.1 | 74.10 |
| Ca(OH)$_2$(aq) | – 1002.8 | 74.10 |
| H$_2$O(l) | – 285.8 | 18.02 |

4. If 170 g of calcium oxide were completely converted into calcium hydroxide via this demonstration reaction, how much heat would be produced?

# Demonstrations

## "The Chef" Worksheet
## Answer Key

Teacher Notes

1. Write a balanced chemical equation for the combination reaction of calcium oxide and water to produce calcium hydroxide. *Hint:* If the solubility of calcium hydroxide in water is only 1.6 g/L, what is the state of the major product?

    $CaO(s) + H_2O(l) \rightarrow Ca(OH)_2(s) + heat$

2. Use Hess's Law to express the heat of reaction for this reaction in terms of the heat of formation of the reactants and products.

    $\Delta H = \Delta H_f(products) - \Delta H_f(reactants)$

    $\Delta H = \Delta H_f[Ca(OH)_2(s)] - \{\Delta H_f[CaO(s)] + \Delta H_f[H_2O(l)]\}$

3. Use the information in the following table to calculate the heat of reaction.

    | Chemical | Heat of Formation (kJ/mole) | Molar Mass (g/mole) |
    |---|---|---|
    | CaO(s) | −635.1 | 56.08 |
    | Ca(OH)$_2$(s) | −986.1 | 74.10 |
    | Ca(OH)$_2$(aq) | −1002.8 | 74.10 |
    | H$_2$O(l) | −285.8 | 18.02 |

    $\Delta H = \Delta H_f[Ca(OH)_2(s)] - \{\Delta H_f[CaO(s)] + \Delta H_f[H_2O(l)]\}$

    $\Delta H = -986.1 \text{ kJ/mol} - (-635.1 \text{ kJ/mol} - 285.8 \text{ kJ/mol})$

    $\Delta H = -65.2 \text{ kJ/mol}$

4. If 170 g of calcium oxide were completely converted into calcium hydroxide via this demonstration reaction, how much heat would be produced?

    $170 \text{ g} \times \left(\dfrac{1 \text{ mole}}{56.0 \text{ g}}\right) \times \left(\dfrac{-65.2 \text{ kJ}}{\text{mole}}\right) = -200 \text{ kJ}$

    *200 kJ of heat would be produced.*

Flinn ChemTopic™ Labs — Chemical Reactions

**Teacher Notes**

# Foiled Again!
## Single Replacement Reaction

### Introduction

Watch aluminum foil disappear as it is added to a solution of copper(II) chloride. Observe color changes, production of a gas, formation of a solid metal, and a drastic change in temperature. Learn about the unexpected role of a catalyst in this single-replacement reaction at a metal surface.

### Concepts

- Single replacement reaction
- Oxidation–reduction
- Metal activity
- Catalysis

### Materials

Aluminum foil, 6″ × 12″, 2 pieces
Copper(II) chloride solution, $CuCl_2$, 1 M, 140 mL
Copper(II) sulfate solution, $CuSO_4$, 1 M, 140 mL
Sodium chloride solution, NaCl, 1 M, 140 mL
Water, distilled or deionized
Beakers, Pyrex®, 600-mL, 3

Graduated cylinder, 500-mL
Spatula
Stirring rod
Thermometer
Wood splint and matches (optional)

### Safety Precautions

*Copper(II) chloride solution is toxic and copper(II) sulfate solution is slightly toxic by ingestion. Hydrogen gas, a highly flammable gas, is produced in the reaction. Keep flammable materials away from the demonstration area. Wear chemical splash goggles and chemical-resistant gloves and apron. Please review current Material Safety Data Sheets for additional safety, handling, and disposal information.*

### Procedure

#### Part 1 — Aluminum and Copper(II) Chloride

1. Place a 600-mL Pyrex® beaker (or a 500-mL graduated cylinder) on the demonstration table.

2. Use a graduated cylinder to measure 140 mL of 1 M copper(II) chloride solution. Pour this into the beaker.

3. Measure and add 140 mL of distilled or deionized water to the beaker. The solution is now 0.5 M $CuCl_2$.

4. Cut a piece of aluminum foil approximately 6″ × 12″. Loosely roll the foil into a cylinder that will fit into the beaker. *Note:* Do not wad up the foil tightly into a ball—this will decrease the surface area and slow down the reaction.

5. If desired, measure the temperature of the solution before adding the foil.

---

*"Foiled Again!" is available as a Chemical Demonstration Kit from Flinn Scientific (Catalog No. AP5936).*

# Demonstrations

6. Place the aluminum foil cylinder into the beaker, using a stirring rod to push it down completely into the solution. Measure the temperature of the reaction mixture again. Notice the great increase in temperature—the reaction is highly exothermic.

7. Have students make detailed observations of the reaction and ask them to generate a hypothesis for the reaction(s) in the beaker. Write an equation for the reaction(s) they observe. Discuss which substances are reacting species and which are spectators in the reaction, if any.

8. Students may hypothesize that aluminum reacts with copper(II) ions to form solid copper and aluminum ions. Test this hypothesis by performing Part 2, in which aluminum is again mixed with copper(II) ions, but this time from a different source, a copper(II) sulfate solution. *Note:* Set the beaker from Part 1 aside for comparison.

### Part 2 — Aluminum and Copper(II) Sulfate

9. Repeat the procedure (steps 1–6) from Part 1 in a different 600-mL beaker, except this time using 70 mL of 1 M $CuSO_4$ solution and 70 mL of distilled or deionized water. The solution is now 0.5 M $CuSO_4$.

10. Have students again make detailed observations. Students will observe that no reaction occurs between aluminum and copper(II) sulfate. Why not? Have students make modifications to this original hypothesis and generate a new hypothesis. Students at this point may propose trying various experiments to test their hypotheses, so additional materials may be needed. *Note:* Set the beaker from Part 2 aside for use in Part 3.

### Part 3 — Aluminum and Copper(II) Sulfate with Sodium Chloride

11. Place the beaker from Part 2 on the demonstration table.

12. Add 70 mL of 1 M NaCl solution to the beaker.

13. Have students make detailed observations. Notice that a reaction now occurs between the aluminum and the copper(II) ions, as in Part 1. Discuss what is occurring in the beaker and write the chemical equation for the reaction. If chloride ions are not in the equation, what is the purpose of the chloride ions? Discuss the role of a catalyst in a reaction.

## Disposal

Please consult your current *Flinn Scientific Catalog/Reference Manual* for general guidelines and specific procedures governing the disposal of laboratory waste. Allow the solid material in the beakers to settle. Decant the copper(II) chloride and copper(II) sulfate solutions down the drain according to Flinn Suggested Disposal Method #26b. Dispose of the solid copper and leftover aluminum foil in the solid waste according to Flinn Suggested Disposal Method #26a.

Teacher Notes

Flinn ChemTopic™ Labs — Chemical Reactions

# Demonstrations

**Teacher Notes**

## Tips

- Test for hydrogen gas with a burning splint: Light a wood splint and hold it in the beaker over the bubbles as they are released from the reaction. A positive test is indicated if a pop or a barking sound is heard. Notice that hydrogen gas is released from the reaction. Discuss the origin of the gas. Write the chemical equation for the production of hydrogen gas.

- The reaction temperature increases from room temperature (25 °C) to nearly 60 °C when aluminum is added to copper(II) chloride. Therefore, be sure to perform the demonstration in Pyrex® glassware.

- Sodium chloride catalyzes the reaction between aluminum and copper(II) sulfate. Observations of the reaction with the catalyst are the same as those observed when aluminum and copper(II) chloride are allowed to react. Other catalysts that have been found to catalyze this reaction include sodium bromide, potassium chloride, magnesium chloride, and hydrochloric acid. It has also been found that copper(II) nitrate reacts in the same way as copper(II) sulfate. As an extension to this demonstration, consider trying other catalysts or other copper solutions.

- Heating the solution of copper(II) sulfate and aluminum to 80 °C does not cause any reaction to occur. The chloride catalyst is necessary for the reaction to occur.

- A more dramatic demonstration display can be achieved by performing the demonstration in large 500-mL Pyrex® graduated cylinders or hydrometer cylinders. Loosely coil the foil into a tube and drop it into the cylinder of $CuCl_2$. The foil will slowly rise in the cylinder as gas bubbles attach to the foil surface. Most of the reaction will occur at the top of the solution (which will turn gray or colorless) and there will be unreacted green-blue copper solution at the bottom of the cylinder. A long stirring rod will be useful in pushing the foil down to the bottom.

- Try using tap water in place of distilled water in the dilution of the $CuSO_4$ solution. Are there enough dissolved chloride ions in tap water to catalyze the reaction?

- The "Leftover Aluminum Wire Stoichiometry Lab" is available as a student laboratory kit from Flinn Scientific (Catalog No. AP4678). This experiment uses the same reaction to teach students about moles, limiting reactants, and stoichiometry.

## Discussion

Aluminum foil reacts with an aqueous solution of copper(II) chloride according to Equation 1. The reaction may be classified as a single replacement, oxidation–reduction reaction.

$$2Al(s) + 3CuCl_2(aq) \rightarrow 2AlCl_3(aq) + 3Cu(s) \qquad \textit{Equation 1}$$
*Silver      Green-blue      Colorless      Red*

The oxidation of aluminum metal to aluminum(III) ions ($Al^0$ to $Al^{3+}$) is inferred from the dissolving of the aluminum foil and is represented by the oxidation half-reaction below. The simultaneous reduction of copper(II) ions to copper metal ($Cu^{2+}$ to $Cu^0$) results in the formation of solid copper metal according to the reduction half-reaction below. As copper(II) ions are reduced to copper, the green-blue color of the solution fades until it is colorless—the indication that the reaction is complete and all of the copper(II) ions have been reduced.

*Foiled Again!*

# Demonstrations

Teacher Notes

$$Al(s) \rightarrow Al^{3+}(aq) + 3e^-  \qquad \text{Oxidation Half-Reaction}$$

$$Cu^{2+}(aq) + 2e^- \rightarrow Cu(s) \qquad \text{Reduction Half-Reaction}$$

$$2Al(s) + 3Cu^{2+}(aq) \rightarrow 2Al^{3+}(aq) + 3Cu(s) \qquad \text{Overall Balanced Equation}$$

It is observed that hydrogen gas is simultaneously released from the reaction when aluminum metal foil is added to copper(II) chloride solution. If the pH of the copper(II) chloride solution is measured, it is found to be slightly acidic. Hence there are free hydrogen ions in solution, which cause the side reaction of hydrogen ions with the aluminum surface to form hydrogen gas and aluminum ions (See Equation 2). Due to the limited concentration of hydrogen ions, this reaction consumes only a small amount of the aluminum.

$$2Al(s) + 6 H^+(aq) \rightarrow 2Al^{3+}(aq) + 3H_2(g) \qquad \textit{Equation 2}$$

Why does aluminum react with copper(II) chloride and not with copper(II) sulfate or copper(II) nitrate? And why does it then react with copper(II) sulfate when chloride ions are added?

This interesting phenomenon was discovered serendipitously by a teacher in the classroom. The teacher wanted to perform the aluminum plus copper(II) chloride reaction with the class, but had run out of copper(II) chloride. Thinking that the net ionic equation should be the same with copper(II) sulfate, the teacher mixed aluminum with cupric sulfate. Nothing happened! After a few grams of salt were added, however, the reaction took off. This was unpredicted and raised a series of questions.

The first possible explanation is that the chloride ions catalyze the reaction at the metal surface. Other halide salts were tried and it was found that bromide ions also catalyzed the reaction. The second possible explanation has to do with the aluminum oxide coating. Normally, a chemically inert coating of aluminum oxide on the surface of aluminum metal protects the metal from oxidation. In the presence of chloride ions, however, the coating is breached and the underlying aluminum reacts. Because chloride is a relatively small ion, it is able to diffuse into and through the protective metal oxide coating. Aluminum chloride, which is more soluble than aluminum oxide, can then form. This aluminum chloride salt leaches back through the oxide coating, and a path is now open for copper(II) ions to attack the underlying metal. The reaction is rapid and extremely exothermic. A third possible explanation for the observations in this demonstration involves electrochemical potentials. The copper–chloride electrode (with copper(II) chloride) has a greater half-cell potential than the copper–copper(II) electrode (with copper(II) sulfate). This supports the observation that the reaction with chloride ions is more favorable than without chloride ions. This experiment is an excellent open-ended demonstration which, like any good inquiry-based lesson, leads to more questions than answers.

**Teacher Notes**

# The Yellow and Blue Switcheroo
## An Oscillating Chemical Reaction

## Introduction

If your students think they have seen it all when it comes to chemical reactions, guess again! Three colorless solutions are mixed to produce a yellow solution that suddenly turns blue, then fades to colorless and turns yellow again. The color of the solution will continue to oscillate between yellow and blue for 10–15 minutes. If you have never performed an oscillating reaction for your students, don't pass this one up—it's a definite show-stopper.

## Concepts

- Oscillating reactions
- Reaction mechanism

## Materials

Hydrogen peroxide, $H_2O_2$, 8.6%, 40 mL

Potassium iodate solution (acidified), $KIO_3$, 0.2 M, 40 mL

Starch–malonic acid–manganous sulfate solution, 40 mL

Beaker, 250-mL

Graduated cylinders, 50-mL, 3

Stirring rod or magnetic stirrer with stir bar

## Safety Precautions

*Hydrogen peroxide is a strong oxidizing agent and a skin and eye irritant. Potassium iodate is also an oxidizer; the solution is acidified and contains sulfuric acid, which is corrosive to eyes, skin and other tissue. Starch–malonic acid–manganous sulfate solution is a strong irritant, moderately toxic, and corrosive to eyes, skin, and the respiratory tract. The reaction produces elemental iodine, which exists in solution, in suspension, and as a vapor above the reaction mixture. The solid iodine is toxic by inhalation. Iodine in solution is irritating to the eyes, skin, and respiratory tract. Perform this demonstration in well-ventilated room. Avoid contact of all chemicals with eyes and skin. Wear chemical splash goggles and chemical-resistant gloves and apron. Please review current Materials Safety Data Sheets for additional safety, handling, and disposal information.*

## Preparation

1. Prepare 8.6% hydrogen peroxide solution by diluting 11.5 mL of 30% hydrogen peroxide to 40 mL with distilled or deionized water.

2. Prepare 0.2 M acidified potassium iodate solution by adding 4 mL of 1 M sulfuric acid to 36 mL distilled water. Add 1.7 g of solid potassium iodate and stir to dissolve.

3. Prepare the starch–malonic acid–manganous sulfate solution by boiling 40 mL of distilled water. Add 0.04 g of soluble starch to about 5 mL of the boiling water. Stir this mixture and add the resulting starch paste to the remaining boiling water. Stir continuously and boil for five minutes. Allow the solution to cool, and then add 0.6 g of malonic acid and 0.16 g of manganous sulfate monohydrate ($MnSO_4 \cdot H_2O$). Stir to dissolve.

*The "Yellow and Blue Switcheroo" is available as a Chemical Demonstration Kit from Flinn Scientific (Catalog No. AP8660).*

The Yellow and Blue Switcheroo

# Demonstrations

## Procedure

1. Using a 50-mL graduated cylinder, measure out 40 mL of 8.6% hydrogen peroxide solution and transfer it to a 250-mL beaker.

2. Using a clean 50-mL graduated cylinder, measure out 40 mL of the acidified 0.2 M potassium iodate solution and add it to the beaker. Stir using a stirring rod or magnetic stirrer.

3. Using the third 50-mL graduated cylinder, measure out 40 mL of the starch–malonic acid–manganous sulfate solution. Add this solution to the beaker and stir.

4. Bubbles will begin to appear. In a short period of time, the solution will turn yellow, then blue, and finally colorless. The entire process will repeat itself over and over again. The yellow to blue to colorless oscillations will continue for about 10 minutes.

## Disposal

Please consult your current *Flinn Scientific Catalog/Reference Manual* for general guidelines and specific procedures governing the disposal of laboratory waste. The reaction mixture may be disposed of by reduction with sodium thiosulfate according to Flinn Suggested Disposal Method #12a.

## Tips

- The reaction can also be done using 3% hydrogen peroxide, although the color changes will not be as sharp. An 8–9% $H_2O$ solution is recommended for this demonstration.

- A magnetic stirrer can be used to stir the solution throughout the entire demonstration or to mix the solutions beforehand. The reaction mixture does not need to be stirred in order to observe the oscillations.

- The demonstration can be done in a Petri dish on an overhead projector. Pour equal amounts (about 5 mL) of each solution into a Petri dish. Swirl the solution to mix. The solution will oscillate between yellow and blue for numerous cycles.

- Use only distilled or deionized water. Chloride ions from tap water may contaminate the reaction mixture and stop the oscillations.

## Discussion

The yellow–blue oscillating reaction is known as the Briggs-Rauscher reaction and was developed by Thomas S. Briggs and Warren C. Rauscher of Galileo High School in San Francisco. The reaction mechanism is very complex. The color changes observed during the reaction are due to oscillations in the concentration of iodine ($I_2$) and iodide ions ($I^-$). The yellow color is attributed to an increase in the $I_2$ concentration. The dark blue color arises from the formation of a starch–iodine complex as both the $I^-$ and $I_2$ concentrations increase. The colorless solution is caused by the decline in $I_2$ concentration and the continued rise in $I^-$ concentration.

amylose

*Teacher Notes*

*This demonstration may be safely scaled up for easy viewing by larger audiences. The oscillating color changes are especially effective if three reaction mixtures are set up simultaneously. With a little luck, the mixtures will exhibit the color changes in quick succession.*

**Teacher Notes**

The dark blue starch–iodine complex consists of amylose–iodine. Amylose is the linear starch fraction which is composed of chains of 1,4-linked α-glucose units as shown on page 82. The color of the complex, blue-black, comes from the pentaiodide anion, $I_5^-$ formed when the $I_2$ and $I^-$ concentrations are elevated. Though normally an unstable anion, $I_5^-$ becomes stable as a part of the starch complex.

The overall Briggs–Rauscher reaction is:

$$IO_3^-(aq) + 2H_2O_2(aq) + CH_2(CO_2H)_2(aq) + H^+(aq) \rightarrow ICH(CO_2H)_2(aq) + 2O_2(g) + 3H_2O(l)$$

The overall reaction may be broken down into two component reactions in which an intermediate compound HOI is generated and then consumed.

$$IO_3^-(aq) + 2H_2O_2(aq) + H^+(aq) \rightarrow HOI(aq) + 2O_2(g) + 2H_2O(l) \qquad \text{Equation 1}$$

$$HOI(aq) + CH_2(CO_2H)_2(aq) \rightarrow ICH(CO_2H)_2(aq) + H_2O(l) \qquad \text{Equation 2}$$

The two component reactions are themselves very complex, consisting of ten steps. Iodine and iodide ions are produced as intermediates in various steps of these reactions.

In the proposed reaction mechanism, the concentration of HOI rises and falls, triggering oscillations in the $I_2$ and $I^-$ concentrations in solution. When the $I_2$ and $I^-$ concentrations are high, the solution is blue; when $I_2$ is high and $I^-$ is low, the solution is yellow; and when $I_2$ is low and $I^-$ is high, the solution is colorless. The oscillations continue until either malonic acid or iodate ions are consumed.

A detailed explanation of the reaction mechanism involves many steps. According to Equation 1, iodate ions are reduced by peroxide to HOI. There are two competing mechanisms for this reaction—a radical mechanism, 1a, and a non-radical one, 1b.

### 1a – Radical Mechanism

i. $2IO_3^- + 2HIO_2 + 2H^+ \rightarrow 4IO_2\cdot + 2H_2O$

ii. $4IO_2\cdot + 4Mn^{2+} + 4H_2O \rightarrow 4HIO_2 + 4Mn(OH)^{2+}$

iii. $4Mn(OH)^{2+} + 4H_2O_2 \rightarrow 4Mn^{2+} + 4H_2O + 4HOO\cdot$

iv. $4HOO\cdot \rightarrow 2H_2O_2 + 2O_2$

v. $2HIO_2 \rightarrow IO_3^- + HOI + H^+$

### 1b – Non-radical Mechanism

i. $IO_3^- + I^- + 2H^+ \rightarrow HIO_2 + HOI$

ii. $HIO_2 + I^- + H^+ \rightarrow 2HOI$

iii. $2HOI + 2H_2O_2 \rightarrow 2I^- + 2O_2 + 2H^+ + 2H_2O$

The Yellow and Blue Switcheroo

# Demonstrations

Equation 2, iodination of malonic acid, takes place by a two-step reaction mechanism.

**Reaction 2 Mechanism**

i. $I^- + HOI + H^+ \rightarrow I_2 + H_2O$

ii. $I_2 + CH_2(CO_2H)_2 \rightarrow ICH(CO_2H)_2 + H^+ + I^-$

When the reactants are mixed, $IO_3^-$ reacts with $H_2O_2$ to produce a small amount of $HIO_2$. Once $HIO_2$ appears, the radical mechanism, 1a, begins. Steps i, ii, and v are fast, resulting in rapid production of hydroiodous acid, HOI. Since reaction 1a is faster than reaction 2 and $[I^-]$ is low, [HOI] builds up. ❶ HOI can now trigger the production of $I^-$ and $I_2$ (see Figure 1).

HOI is reduced by $H_2O_2$, (reaction iii of 1b), to produce $I^-$. As $[I^-]$ increases, ❷, HOI reacts with $I^-$, (reaction i of 2), to form $I_2$. At this point, the solution is still clear, since $I_2$ concentration is still low.

Now, HOI, $I^-$, and $I_2$ concentrations all continue to increase. As $[I^-]$ increases, its reaction rate with $HIO_2$, (ii of 1b) exceeds the rate for radical steps i and ii and the radical process shuts off. Now $[I^-]$ and $[I_2]$ are high and the solution turns blue. ❸

The non-radical process, along with the first step of reaction 2, depletes both $I^-$ and HOI. As $[I_2]$ builds up, the solution turns yellow. ❹ Once $[I^-]$ and [HOI] are low enough, $[I_2]$ drops as malonic acid converts it in step ii of reaction 2.

At low $[I^-]$, the rate for steps i and ii of the radical reaction mechanism exceed that for step i of the non-radical one and the radical mechanism takes over. When $[I_2]$ is low enough, the solution clears. ❺ The process repeats itself and the oscillations continue until either malonic acid or iodate is consumed.

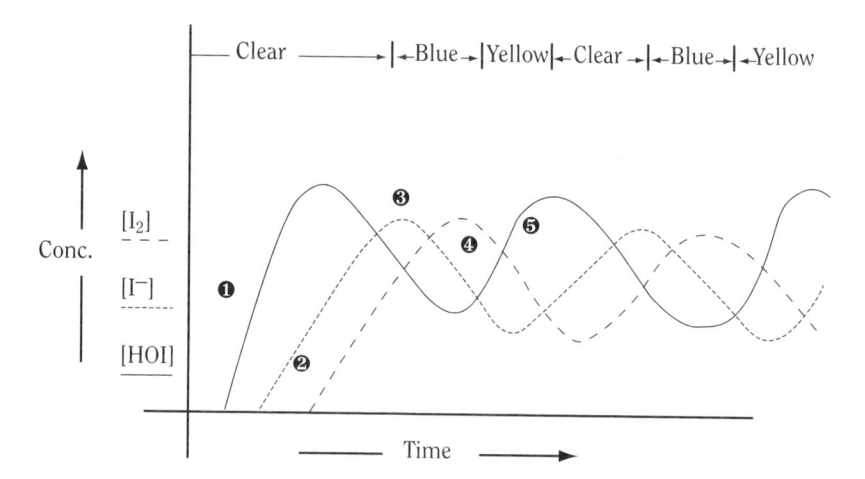

**Figure 1.** Color oscillations in the Yellow–Blue Switcheroo.

**Teacher Notes**

# Old Foamey
## Decomposition of Hydrogen Peroxide

### Introduction

Bubbles and heat, steam and foam, "Old Foamey" has it all! Mix hydrogen peroxide with dishwashing liquid, add sodium iodide catalyst, then stand back and observe the decomposition reaction as it erupts in a wall of cascading foam.

### Concepts

- Decomposition reaction
- Catalyst

### Materials

Hydrogen peroxide, 30%, $H_2O_2$, 20 mL
Sodium iodide solution, 2 M, KI, 5 mL
Dishwashing liquid (Dove®), 10 mL
Food coloring (optional)

Graduated cylinder, Pyrex®, 100-mL
Graduated cylinder, 10-mL
Plastic demonstration tray
Wood splint (optional)

### Safety Precautions

*Hydrogen peroxide is a strong oxidizing agent; it is severely corrosive to the skin, eyes and respiratory tract and is a dangerous fire and explosion risk. Do not heat this substance. Sodium iodide is slightly toxic by ingestion. Do not stand over the reaction mixture—the heat and steam produced can be very intense. Wear chemical splash goggles and chemical-resistant gloves and apron. Please review current Material Safety Data Sheets for additional safety, handling, and disposal imformation.*

### Procedure

1. Place a 100-mL graduated cylinder on a plastic demonstration tray that is several inches deep.

2. Measure out 20 mL of the 30% hydrogen peroxide into the 100-mL graduated cylinder.

3. Measure out 10 mL of dishwashing liquid into the 10-mL graduated cylinder and add it to the cylinder containing the hydrogen peroxide. Add a few drops of food coloring, if desired. Observe that little or no reaction occurs in the absence of a catalyst.

4. Measure out 5 mL of sodium iodide solution into the 10-mL graduated cylinder. Quickly but carefully add the sodium iodide solution to the hydrogen peroxide–dishwashing liquid mixture in the large graduated cylinder.

5. *(Optional)* Light a wood splint and blow out the flame to produce a glowing splint. Insert the glowing splint in the foam—it will reignite.

*"Old Foamey" is available as a Chemical Demonstration Kit from Flinn Scientific (Catalog No. AP2085).*

# Demonstrations

## Disposal

Please consult your current *Flinn Scientific Catalog/Reference Manual* for general guidelines and specific procedures governing the disposal of laboratory waste. The leftover foam and solution in the cylinder may be rinsed down the drain with excess water according to Flinn Suggested Disposal Method #26b.

## Tips

- The decomposition reaction produces lots of foam—so much that this demonstration is often called "Elephant's Toothpaste." Carry out the demonstration in a large plastic demonstration tray or, if none is available, in the laboratory sink. Cleanup, at least, is easy because of the generous amount of dishwashing liquid used.

- The decomposition reaction is highly exothermic. Carry out the reaction in heat-resistant, borosilicate (e.g., Pyrex®) glassware and check all glassware for chips or cracks before use. Allow the glassware to cool before disposing of the reaction mixture.

- This demonstration can be scaled up for larger audiences. A 500-mL or 1-L Pyrex® graduated cylinder works well with about 100 mL of hydrogen peroxide. The amount of dishwashing liquid and catalyst solution do *not* have to be increased proportionally.

- A slight brown tinge is observed at the edge of the foam at the beginning of the reaction. The yellow-brown color is due to the presence of free iodine produced by the oxidation of the catalyst, sodium iodide. The yellow color disappears when the catalyst is regenerated.

- Other catalysts that will catalyze this reaction include manganese(IV) oxide, $MnO_2$, and manganese metal, Mn.

## Discussion

The decomposition reaction of hydrogen peroxide is highly exothermic and produces lots of heat and steam. The action of a catalyst is demonstrated through the use of sodium iodide, which speeds up the decomposition reaction. The products of the reaction are water vapor and oxygen gas. The presence of oxygen gas in the foam is demonstrated by the glowing splint test. When a glowing splint is inserted into the foam, it spontaneously reignites due to the increased concentration of oxygen.

$$2H_2O_2(aq) \xrightarrow{I^-(aq)} 2H_2O(g) + O_2(g) + \text{Energy}$$

Teacher Notes

# Demonstrations

**Teacher Notes**

# Cool Light
## Chemiluminescence Reaction

### Introduction

Chemiluminescence demonstrations are popular with students and teachers alike. This demonstration illustrates the light-producing reaction that takes place when luminol is oxidized.

### Concepts

- Chemiluminescence
- Oxidation–reduction

### Materials

Luminol, 0.1 g

Sodium hydroxide solution, 1 M, NaOH, 65 mL

Potassium ferricyanide, $K_3Fe(CN)_6$, 0.7 g

Hydrogen peroxide, $H_2O_2$, 3%, 15 mL

Water, distilled or deionized

Beakers, 1-L, 2

Erlenmeyer flask, 2-L

Funnel, large

Graduated cylinder, 50-mL

Ring stand and ring

Spatula

Stirring rod, plastic

### Safety Precautions

*Hydrogen peroxide is an oxidizing agent and a skin and eye irritant. Sodium hydroxide solution is a corrosive liquid; skin burns are possible. Potassium ferricyanide is slightly toxic by ingestion; heating to decomposition or contact with concentrated acids may evolve poisonous hydrogen cyanide. Wear chemical splash goggles and chemical-resistant gloves and apron. Please review current Material Safety Data Sheets for additional safety, handling, and disposal information.*

### Preparation

1. Prepare Solution A by adding 0.1 g of luminol and 65 mL of 1 M sodium hydroxide solution to approximately 800 mL of distilled or deionized water. Stir to dissolve the luminol.

2. Prepare Solution B by adding 0.7 g of potassium ferricyanide and 15 mL of 3% hydrogen peroxide to approximately 800 mL of DI water. Stir to dissolve the potassium ferricyanide.

3. Set up the demonstration equipment as shown in Figure 1.

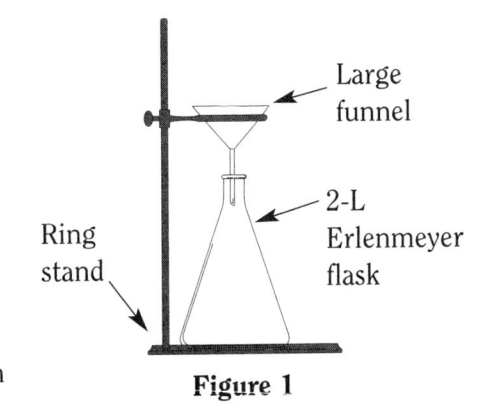

**Figure 1**

### Procedure

1. Turn down the lights and pull the shades or drapes if possible—the demonstration is most effective in a very dark room.

2. Simultaneously pour Solution A and Solution B into the large funnel. As the two solutions mix, chemiluminescence begins. (The solution will give off a "cool blue" light.)

---

*"Cool Light" is available as a Chemical Demonstration Kit from Flinn Scientific (Catalog No. AP8627). The most common problem with this demonstration is that students cannot see the blue light due to the room not being dark enough. Get the room as dark as possible for a successful and awe-inspiring demonstration.*

Cool Light

# Demonstrations

Teacher Notes

3. As the reaction progresses, it can be enhanced by adding small amounts of potassium ferricyanide and 5–10 mL of 1 M sodium hydroxide solution into the flask.

## Disposal

Consult your current *Flinn Scientific Catalog/Reference Manual* for general guidelines and specific procedures governing the disposal of laboratory waste. The final solution may be disposed of down the drain with plenty of excess water according to Flinn Suggested Disposal Method #26b.

## Tips

- This demonstration is especially appealing if it is set up so the students can see the mixture through clear plastic, spiral tubing. See the directions for setup at the end of the *Discussion* section. This type of apparatus gives a large surface area for light to be emitted and provides a flowing effect which increases the overall visual impact.

- Use only distilled or deionized water when preparing the solutions. Hard water and softened water may contain high concentrations of ions (such as chloride ions) that will interfere with the excited state of the luminol and prevent chemiluminescence.

## Discussion

Chemiluminescence is defined as the production or emission of light that accompanies a chemical reaction. Light emission results from the conversion of chemical energy into light energy due to changes in the composition of a chemiluminescent material. The "flame test" colors observed when different metal salts are burned in a Bunsen burner flame are examples of a type of chemiluminescence known as pyroluminescence. The glow of solid phosphorus in air is another classic example of chemiluminescence—light, along with some heat, is produced when the phosphorus undergoes an oxidation reaction. The oxidation of luminol (3-aminophthalhydrazide) in this demonstration illustrates a type of "cool light" chemiluminescence in which little or no heat is produced.

The light-producing chemical reactions of luminol were discovered by H. O. Albrecht in 1928. Since that time numerous procedures have been developed to produce light using luminol. Experiments have shown that the following "ingredients" are necessary for luminol to exhibit chemiluminescence—a basic (alkaline) pH, an oxidizing agent, and a catalyst. In this demonstration, the oxidizing agent is hydrogen peroxide, the catalyst is the iron(III) cation in potassium ferricyanide, and sodium hydroxide is used to maintain the basic pH needed for the reaction to occur.

Oxidation of luminol and the resulting chemiluminscence occurs in the following sequence of reactions:

(1) Sodium hydroxide acts as a base and converts luminol (structure I) into a dianion.

(2) Hydrogen peroxide oxidizes the dianion form of luminol to the aminophthalate ion (structure II), which is produced in an excited electronic state.

(3) The excited aminophthalate ion decays to a lower energy ground state and gives off light in the process. The emitted light has a wavelength of 425 nm, which is in the blue region of the visible spectrum.

*Flinn ChemTopic™ Labs* — Chemical Reactions

# Demonstrations

**Teacher Notes**

[Chemical reaction: Luminol (I) with amino group and two NH groups in the phthalazinedione ring + 2OH⁻ + $H_2O_2$ → 3-aminophthalate dianion (II) + $2H_2O$ + $N_2$]

## Make Your Own "Cool Light" Spiral Apparatus

### Materials

Glass funnel (large enough to sit in the opening of the Plexiglas tube)
Clear plastic (Tygon®) tubing, 6 ft
Long Plexiglas® tube
Glass elbows or glass tubing with bends, 2
Collecting flask, battery jar or beaker, 2-L
Electric drill

1. Attach a small piece of plastic tubing, a glass elbow, and the long plastic tubing to the funnel stem. Place the funnel with attached tubing into the Plexiglas tube.

2. Drill a hole in the Plexiglas tube just below the height of the glass elbow connected to the funnel stem. Thread the long plastic tubing through this hole from the inside out.

3. Spiral the tubing around the outside of the Plexiglas tube.

4. Drill a hole in the Plexiglas tube 1" above the height of the collecting flask. Feed the spiraled tubing through the hole and attach it to a glass elbow and a small piece of plastic tubing. If the tubing does not stay tightly spiraled, a small amount of quick-drying glue can be used to keep it in place.

5. Select a collecting flask (e.g., battery jar, beaker) large enough to contain the total volume of liquid used in the demonstration. The Plexiglas tube must fit over the outside of the flask. Insert the plastic tubing into the collecting flask.

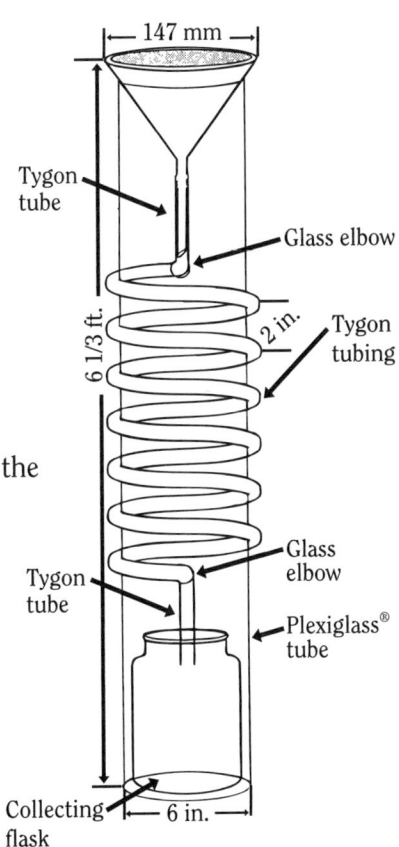

6. Depending on the height of the Plexiglass® tube and spiral tubing, build a support stand or attach the tube to a ring stand for stability. This will prevent the apparatus from tipping over.

7. Once the apparatus is set up, dim the lights and pour the demonstration solutions through the funnel. Your students will love the special effects!

Cool Light

**Safety and Disposal**

# Safety and Disposal Guidelines

## Safety Guidelines

Teachers owe their students a duty of care to protect them from harm and to take reasonable precautions to prevent accidents from occurring. A teacher's duty of care includes the following:

- Supervising students in the classroom.
- Providing adequate instructions for students to perform the tasks required of them.
- Warning students of the possible dangers involved in performing the activity.
- Providing safe facilities and equipment for the performance of the activity.
- Maintaining laboratory equipment in proper working order.

## Safety Contract

The first step in creating a safe laboratory environment is to develop a safety contract that describes the rules of the laboratory for your students. Before a student ever sets foot in a laboratory, the safety contract should be reviewed and then signed by the student and a parent or guardian. Please contact Flinn Scientific at 800-452-1261 or visit the Flinn Website at www.flinnsci.com to request a free copy of the Flinn Scientific Safety Contract.

To fulfill your duty of care, observe the following guidelines:

1. **Be prepared.** Practice all experiments and demonstrations beforehand. Never perform a lab activity if you have not tested it, if you do not understand it, or if you do not have the resources to perform it safely.

2. **Set a good example.** The teacher is the most visible and important role model. Wear your safety goggles whenever you are working in the lab, even (or especially) when class is not in session. Students learn from your good example—whether you are preparing reagents, testing a procedure, or performing a demonstration.

3. **Maintain a safe lab environment.** Provide high-quality goggles that offer adequate protection and are comfortable to wear. Make sure there is proper safety equipment in the laboratory and that it is maintained in good working order. Inspect all safety equipment on a regular basis to ensure its readiness.

4. **Start with safety.** Incorporate safety into each laboratory exercise. Begin each lab period with a discussion of the properties of the chemicals or procedures used in the experiment and any special precautions—including goggle use—that must be observed. Pre-lab assignments are an ideal mechanism to ensure that students are prepared for lab and understand the safety precautions. Record all safety instruction in your lesson plan.

5. **Proper instruction.** Demonstrate new or unusual laboratory procedures before every activity. Instruct students on the safe way to handle chemicals, glassware, and equipment.

6. **Supervision.** Never leave students unattended—always provide adequate supervision. Work with school administrators to make sure that class size does not exceed the capacity of the room or your ability to maintain a safe lab environment. Be prepared and alert to what students are doing so that you can prevent accidents before they happen.

7. **Understand your resources.** Know yourself, your students, and your resources. Use discretion in choosing experiments and demonstrations that match your background and fit within the knowledge and skill level of your students and the resources of your classroom. You are the best judge of what will work or not. Do not perform any activities that you feel are unsafe, that you are uncomfortable performing, or that you do not have the proper equipment for.

## Safety Precautions

*Specific safety precautions have been written for every experiment and demonstration in this book. The safety information describes the hazardous nature of each chemical and the specific precautions that must be followed to avoid exposure or accidents. The safety section also alerts you to potential dangers in the procedure or techniques. Regardless of what lab program you use, it is important to maintain a library of current Material Safety Data Sheets for all chemicals in your inventory. Please consult current MSDS for additional safety, handling, and disposal information.*

## Disposal Procedures

The disposal procedures included in this book are based on the Suggested Laboratory Chemical Disposal Procedures found in the *Flinn Scientific Catalog/Reference Manual*. The disposal procedures are only suggestions—do not use these procedures without first consulting with your local government regulatory officials.

Many of the experiments and demonstrations produce small volumes of aqueous solutions that can be flushed down the drain with excess water. Do not use this procedure if your drains empty into groundwater through a septic system or into a storm sewer. Local regulations may be more strict on drain disposal than the practices suggested in this book and in the *Flinn Scientific Catalog/Reference Manual*. You must determine what types of disposal procedures are permitted in your area—contact your local authorities.

Any suggested disposal method that includes "discard in the trash" requires your active attention and involvement. Make sure that the material is no longer reactive, is placed in a suitable container (plastic bag or bottle), and is in accordance with local landfill regulations. Please do not inadvertently perform any extra "demonstrations" due to unpredictable chemical reactions occurring in your trash can. Think before you throw!

Finally, please read all the narratives before you attempt any Suggested Laboratory Chemical Disposal Procedure found in your current *Flinn Scientific Catalog/Reference Manual*.

Flinn Scientific is your most trusted and reliable source of reference, safety, and disposal information for all chemicals used in the high school science lab. To request a complimentary copy of the most recent *Flinn Scientific Catalog/Reference Manual,* call us at 800-452-1261 or visit our Web site at www.flinnsci.com.

# National Science Education Standards

## Experiments and Demonstrations

| Content Standards | Classifying Chemical Reactions | Double Replacement Reactions | A Four-Reaction Copper Cycle | Chemical Reactions & Qualitative Analysis | Chemical Reactions Primer | Colorful Electrolysis | The Chef | Foiled Again! | The Yellow and Blue Switcheroo | Old Foamey | Cool Light |
|---|---|---|---|---|---|---|---|---|---|---|---|
| **Unifying Concepts and Processes** | | | | | | | | | | | |
| Systems, order, and organization | ✓ | ✓ | ✓ | ✓ | ✓ | ✓ | ✓ | ✓ | ✓ | ✓ | ✓ |
| Evidence, models, and explanation | ✓ | ✓ | ✓ | ✓ | ✓ | ✓ | ✓ | ✓ | ✓ | ✓ | ✓ |
| Constancy, change, and measurement | | | | | | | | | | | |
| Evolution and equilibrium | | | | | | | | | | | |
| Form and function | | | | | | | | | | | |
| **Science as Inquiry** | | | | | | | | | | | |
| Identify questions and concepts that guide scientific investigation | ✓ | ✓ | | ✓ | ✓ | | | | | | |
| Design and conduct scientific investigations | ✓ | ✓ | | ✓ | | | | | | | |
| Use technology and mathematics to improve scientific investigations | | | | | | | | | | | |
| Formulate and revise scientific explanations and models using logic and evidence | ✓ | ✓ | | ✓ | ✓ | ✓ | | ✓ | ✓ | ✓ | |
| Recognize and analyze alternative explanations and models | | ✓ | | | | | | | | | |
| Communicate and defend a scientific argument | | | | ✓ | | | | | | | |
| Understand scientific inquiry | ✓ | ✓ | | ✓ | ✓ | | | | | | |
| **Physical Science** | | | | | | | | | | | |
| Structure of atoms | | | | | | | | | | | |
| Structure and properties of matter | ✓ | ✓ | ✓ | ✓ | ✓ | ✓ | ✓ | ✓ | ✓ | ✓ | ✓ |
| Chemical reactions | ✓ | ✓ | ✓ | ✓ | ✓ | ✓ | ✓ | ✓ | ✓ | ✓ | ✓ |
| Motions and forces | | | | | | | | | | | |
| Conservation of energy and the increase in disorder | | | | | | | | | | | |
| Interactions of energy and matter | ✓ | | ✓ | | ✓ | ✓ | ✓ | ✓ | | ✓ | ✓ |

Flinn ChemTopic™ Labs — Chemical Reactions

**National Science Education Standards**

## Content Standards *(continued)*

**Experiments and Demonstrations**

| | Classifying Chemical Reactions | Double Replacement Reactions | A Four-Reaction Copper Cycle | Chemical Reactions & Qualitative Analysis | Chemical Reactions Primer | Colorful Electrolysis | The Chef | Foiled Again! | The Yellow and Blue Switcheroo | Old Foamey | Cool Light |
|---|---|---|---|---|---|---|---|---|---|---|---|
| **Science and Technology** | | | | | | | | | | | |
| Identify a problem or design an opportunity | | | | | | | | | | | |
| Propose designs and choose between alternative solutions | | | | ✓ | | | | | | | |
| Implement a proposed solution | | | | ✓ | | | | | | | |
| Evaluate the solution and its consequences | | | | ✓ | | | | | | | |
| Communicate the problem, process, and solution | | | | | | | | | | | |
| Understand science and technology | ✓ | ✓ | ✓ | ✓ | ✓ | ✓ | ✓ | ✓ | ✓ | ✓ | ✓ |
| **Science in Personal and Social Perspectives** | | | | | | | | | | | |
| Personal and community health | | | | ✓ | | | | | | | |
| Population growth | | | | | | | | | | | |
| Natural resources | | | ✓ | | | | | | | | |
| Environmental quality | | | | ✓ | | | | | | | |
| Natural and human-induced hazards | | | | | | | | | | | |
| Science and technology in local, national, and global challenges | | | | | | | | | | | |
| **History and Nature of Science** | | | | | | | | | | | |
| Science as a human endeavor | | | | | | | | | | | |
| Nature of scientific knowledge | ✓ | ✓ | ✓ | ✓ | | | | | | | |
| Historical perspectives | | | | | | | | | | | |

National Science Education Standards

# Master Materials Guide

*(for a class of 30 students working in pairs)*

### Experiments and Demonstrations

| Chemicals | Flinn Scientific Catalog No. | Classifying Chemical Reactions | Double Replacement Reactions | A Four-Reaction Copper Cycle | Chemical Reactions & Qualitative Analysis | Chemical Reactions Primer | Colorful Electrolysis | The Chef | Foiled Again! | The Yellow and Blue Switcheroo | Old Foamey | Cool Light |
|---|---|---|---|---|---|---|---|---|---|---|---|---|
| Acetone | A0009 | | | 150 mL | | | | | | | | |
| Aluminum foil | A0019 | | | | | | | | 1 | | | |
| Aluminum nitrate solution, 0.1 M | A0277 | | 30 mL | | | | | | | | | |
| Ammonium carbonate | A0226 | 7 g | | | | | | | | | | |
| Ammonium hydroxide solution, 6 M | A0192 | | | | 50 mL | 5 mL | | | | | | |
| Ammonium nitrate | A0241 | | 1 g | | | | | | | | | |
| Barium nitrate solution, 0.1 M | B0148 | | 30 mL | | | | | | | | | |
| Bromcresol green solution, 0.04% | B0064 | | | | | 1 mL | | | | | | |
| Calcium carbonate | C0347 | 7 g | | | | | | | | | | |
| Calcium nitrate solution, 0.1 M | C0236 | | 30 mL | | | | | | | | | |
| Calcium oxide, lump | C0028 | | | | | | | 200 g | | | | |
| Copper powder | C0086 | | | 5 g | | | | | | | | |
| Cupric chloride dihydrate | C0212 | 9 g | | | | 5 g | | | 26 g | | | |
| Cupric nitrate solution, 0.1 M | C0245 | | 30 mL | | | | | | | | | |
| Cupric sulfate solution, 1 M | C0246 | | | | | | | 140 mL | | | | |
| Ethyl alcohol | E0007 | 25 mL | | | | 1 mL | | | | | | |
| Ferric chloride solution, 1 M | F0069 | | | | | 5 mL | | | | | | |
| Ferric nitrate | F0008 | | | | 6 g | | | | | | | |
| Ferric nitrate solution, 0.1 M | F0047 | | 30 mL | | | | | | | | | |
| Hydrochloric acid, 3 M | H0034 | | | 375 mL | 50 mL | 10 mL | | | | | | |
| Hydrochloric acid, 1 M | H0013 | 75 mL | | | | | | | | | | |
| Hydrogen peroxide, 30% | H0037 | | | | | | | | | 12 mL | 20 mL | |
| Hydrogen peroxide solution, 6% | H0028 | | | | | 5 mL | | | | | | |
| Hydrogen peroxide solution, 3% | H0009 | | | | | | | | | | | 15 mL |
| Iron wire, 18 gauge | I0050 | | | | | 4 cm | | | | | | |
| Luminol | L0031 | | | | | | | | | | | 1 g |
| Magnesium ribbon | M0139 | 1.5 m | | | | | | | | | | |
| Magnesium turnings | M0112 | | | 10 g | | | | | | | | |
| Malonic acid | M0091 | | | | | | | | | 1 g | | |
| Manganous sulfate | M0030 | | | | | | | | | 1 g | | |
| Nitric acid solution, 6 M | N0048 | | | 100 mL | | | | | | | | |
| Phenolphthalein solution, 1% | P0019 | 5 mL | | | | | | | | | | |
| Phenol red solution, 0.02% | P0100 | | | | | 1 mL | | | | | | |
| Potassium ferricyanide | P0050 | | | | | | | | | | | 1 g |
| Potassium ferrocyanide | P0053 | | | | 5 g | | | | | | | |
| Potassium iodate | P0063 | | | | | | | | | | 2 g | |

# Master Materials Guide

*(for a class of 30 students working in pairs)*

**Experiments and Demonstrations**

| | Flinn Scientific Catalog No. | Classifying Chemical Reactions | Double Replacement Reactions | A Four-Reaction Copper Cycle | Chemical Reactions & Qualitative Analysis | Chemical Reactions Primer | Colorful Electrolysis | The Chef | Foiled Again! | The Yellow and Blue Switcheroo | Old Foamey | Cool Light |
|---|---|---|---|---|---|---|---|---|---|---|---|---|
| **Chemicals, continued** | | | | | | | | | | | | |
| Potassium thiocyanate | P0225 | | | 1 g | | | | | | | | |
| Silver nitrate solution, 0.1 M | S0305 | | 30 mL | | | | | | | | | |
| Sodium carbonate solution, 0.1 M | S0235 | | 45 mL | | | | | | | | | |
| Sodium chloride | S0061 | | | | | | 20 g | | 2 g | | | |
| Sodium chloride solution, 0.1 M | S0237 | | 45 mL | | | | | | | | | |
| Sodium hydroxide solution, 6 M | S0242 | | | 100 mL | 50 mL | | | | | | | |
| Sodium hydroxide solution, 1 M | S0148 | 25 mL | | | | 5 mL | | | | | | 65 mL |
| Sodium hydroxide solution, 0.1 M | S0149 | | 45 mL | | | | | | | | | |
| Sodium iodide | S0218 | | | | | | | | | | 2 g | |
| Sodium iodide solution, 0.1 M | S0245 | | 45 mL | | | | | | | | | |
| Sodium phosphate, tribasic | S0101 | 10 g | | 29 g | | 5 g | | | | | | |
| Sodium phosphate, tribasic, solution, 0.1 M | S0250 | | 45 mL | | | | | | | | | |
| Sodium sulfate solution, 0.1 M | S0251 | | 45 mL | | | | | | | | | |
| Starch | S0122 | | | | | | | | | | 1 g | |
| Sulfur | S0142 | | | | 1 g | | | | | | | |
| Sulfuric acid, 1 M | S0202 | | | | 2 mL | | | | 4 mL | | | |
| Universal indicator solution | U0001 | | | | | | 100 mL | | | | | |
| Yeast, Baker's | Y0008 | | | | | 1 g | | | | | | |
| Zinc, mossy | Z0003 | 55 g | | | 9 g | | | | | | | |
| Zinc nitrate solution, 0.1 M | Z0026 | | 30 mL | | | | | | | | | |
| **Glassware** | | | | | | | | | | | | |
| Beaker, 50-mL | GP1005 | | | 15 | | | | | | | | |
| Beaker, 250-mL | GP1020 | | | 15 | | | | | 1 | | | |
| Beaker, 600-mL | GP1030 | | | | | | | | 3 | | | |
| Beaker, 1-L | GP1040 | | | | | | 1 | | | | | 2 |
| Erlenmeyer flask, 125-mL | GP3040 | | | 30 | | | | | | | | |
| Erlenmeyer flask, 250-mL | GP3045 | | | | 1 | | | | | | | |
| Erlenmeyer flask, 2-L | GP9155 | | | | | | | | | | | 1 |
| Funnel | GP5045 | | | 15 | | | | | | | | |
| Graduated cylinder, 10-mL | GP2005 | | | 15 | 5 | | | | | | 1 | |
| Graduated cylinder, 25-mL | GP2010 | | | 15 | | | | | | | | |
| Graduated cylinder, 50-mL | GP2015 | | | | | | | | | 3 | | 1 |
| Graduated cylinder, 100-mL | GP2020 | | | | | | | | | | 1 | |
| Graduated cylinder, 500-mL | GP2030 | | | | | | | | 1 | | | |

*Continued on next page*

# Master Materials Guide

*(for a class of 30 students working in pairs)*

**Experiments and Demonstrations**

| | Flinn Scientific Catalog No. | Classifying Chemical Reactions | Double Replacement Reactions | A Four-Reaction Copper Cycle | Chemical Reactions & Qualitative Analysis | Chemical Reactions Primer | Colorful Electrolysis | The Chef | Foiled Again! | The Yellow and Blue Switcheroo | Old Foamey | Cool Light |
|---|---|---|---|---|---|---|---|---|---|---|---|---|
| **Glassware, continued** | | | | | | | | | | | | |
| Petri dish with cover | GP3019 | | | | | 1 | | | | | | |
| Stirring rod | GP5075 | | 15 | 15 | | 1 | | | 1 | 1 | | 1 |
| Test tube, 13 × 100 mm | GP6063 | 90 | | | 90 | | | | | | | |
| Test tube, 16 × 150 mm | GP6066 | | | | | 7 | | | | | | |
| **General Equipment and Miscellaneous** | | | | | | | | | | | | |
| Balance, centigram (0.01-g precision) | OB2059 | | | 3 | | | | | 1 | 1 | | 1 |
| Battery, 9-V | AP1430 | | | | | | 1 | | | | | |
| Battery clip with alligator ends | AP8945 | | | | | | 1 | | | | | |
| Bunsen burner | AP5344 | 15 | | | | 1 | | | | | | |
| Butane safety lighter | AP8960 | 3 | | | | 1 | | | | | | |
| Centrifuge | AP8710 | | | | 1 | | | | | | | |
| Ceramic fiber squares | AP1240 | 15 | | | | 1 | | | | | | |
| Deflagration spoon | AP1346 | | | | | 1 | | | | | | |
| Evaporating dish, porcelain | AP1272 | 15 | | 15 | | 1 | | | | | | |
| Filter paper, quantitative, 11-cm | AP8997 | | | 15 | | | | | | | | |
| Forceps, specimen | AB1093 | 15 | | | | | | | | | | |
| Funnel, utility | AP3202 | | | | | | | | | | | 1 |
| Hot plate | AP4674 | | | 5 | | | | | | | | |
| Litmus paper, neutral | AP7934 | 1 | | | | | | | | | | |
| pH paper | AP1107 | | | 1 | | | | | | | | |
| Pipet, Beral-type, graduated | AP1721 | 90 | | 60 | 150 | 5 | | | | | | |
| Pipet, thin-stem | AP1444 | | 210 | | | | | | | | | |
| Reaction plate, 24-well | AP1447 | | 15 | | | | | | | | | |
| Reaction plate, 96-well | AP1448 | | 15 | | | | | | | | | |
| Ring support, 4" | AP8232 | | | | | | | | | | | 1 |
| Rubber stopper, size 00 | AP2219 | | | | 30 | | | | | | | |
| Spatula | AP1323 | 15 | | 15 | | 1 | | | 1 | 1 | | |
| Support stand, 6" x 9" | AP8228 | | | | | | | | | | | 1 |
| Test tube clamp | AP8217 | 15 | | | | 1 | | | | | | |
| Test tube rack | AP1319 | 15 | | | 15 | | | | | | | |
| Wash bottle | AP1668 | 15 | 15 | 15 | 15 | | 1 | | | | | |
| Water, distilled or deionized | W0007 | ✓ | ✓ | ✓ | ✓ | ✓ | ✓ | ✓ | ✓ | ✓ | | ✓ |
| Weighing dishes | AP1278 | | | 15 | | | | | | | | |
| Wood splints | AP4455 | 45 | | | | 2 | | | 1 | 1 | | |